DARLEY

THE MOST POPULAR ILLUSTRATOR OF HIS TIME

A PICTURE OF F. O. C. DARLEY

(from *Harper's Weekly*, 1867)

DARLEY

The Most Popular Illustrator of His Time

by ETHEL KING

Published by

THEO. GAUS' SONS, INC.
Brooklyn 1, N. Y.

FELIX OCTAVIUS CARR DARLEY
THE MOST POPULAR ILLUSTRATOR
OF HIS TIME

"Jarvis tried but failed to embody my conception of Diedrich Knickerbocker; Leslie also. Darley hit it in the *Illustrated History of New York*. My idea was that he should carry the air of one profoundly impressed with the truth of his own history."
—*Washington Irving*

ACKNOWLEDGMENTS

Grateful thanks to:

The New York Times
The New York Public Library
The New-York Historical Society
The Society Library
The Museum of the City of New York
Frick Art Reference Library
The National Academy of Design
Putnam's & Coward-McCann
The Philadelphia Chamber of Commerce
The Historical Society of Pennsylvania
The Philadelphia Museum of Art Library

CONTENTS

LIST OF ILLUSTRATIONS BY F. O. C. DARLEY

DARLEY

THE MOST POPULAR ILLUSTRATOR
OF HIS TIME

CHAPTER I

Genesis

ILLUSTRATED BY DARLEY! Those were magic words in the 1850's and 1860's in the advertisement of a new book. Prosperity was awakening the American public to the knowledge of books. So they bought books, and read them. Books, well-written, well-bound, and well illustrated, were highly prized. Many who purchased such books felt possession a sign of standing, while to the more fastidious books of this type proved a delightful necessity.

F. O. C. Darley, as he often signed himself, was an artist perhaps best known for his illustrations. Webster's Dictionary gives the following definitions for the charming word, *illustrate*: 1. (Archaic) To enlighten: illuminate. 2. (Obs.) To make illustrious. 3. (Obs.) To make luminous; to light up. 4. To make clear; to explain, as by figures and examples. 5. To provide with pictures or designs for elucidation or adornment; of pictures, etc., to elucidate or adorn.

Darley was an artist, and therefore could both adorn and explain deftly the works he illustrated. He was largely self-taught, but, as background, he had parents who were actors. In all probability he inherited from them a sense of drama, and the gift of character reading and impersonation. Shakespeare was an actor and his knowledge of the stage added to genius made him a master dramatist. He could inform and inspire, and Darley, in his own way, could do the same.

Darley was of British origin, as both parents were English. But there might even have been some Irish in him, for a George Darley (1795-1846), born in Dublin, became in time both poet and mathematician—an odd combination of endeavors. His poems were mostly dramatic in nature, such as: Errors of Ecstasie (1822), and Labors of Idleness (1826), etc. (World Encyclopedia.)

Felix Octavius Carr Darley was the poet's full name. Long names were in style then, such as: James Fenimore Cooper; John Greenleaf Whittier; Edward Everett Hale. George Gordon Noel Byron, etc. And this custom did not imply pomposity, but rather deep affection for family and friends. When parents called a child in honor of a relative or some dear one, it showed thought, or in a name or names added later, meant respect for the name or names adopted.

So, Felix Octavius Carr Darley was born in 1822, and lived busily until 1888, not a very long life, but a fruitful one. Can any conclusions be drawn from his names, and usually he employed simply initials for the first three: F. O. C. Darley. Well, Felix certainly means happy, and he must have been so blessed, for his pictures and his writings indicate a man of sense and feeling, and therefore a happy one. Octavius might have indicated he was the eighth child of the union, or just a memory of the Roman plays of Shakespeare. And as for Carr, some dear friend or benefactor must have been the cause for the bestowal of that appellation. The cognomen, Darley, was the family name. The old Romans usually had three names: praenomen, nomen, cognomen. And the agnomen, an additional name, was given to commemorate some achievement.

The father of this famous son, John Darley, had been a comedian—and does not that explain how the son could put humor into his pictures? This was an inheritance. His mother, Eleanor Westray, at one time was a popular actress. These two people came to America, and were married here in 1800. At that time John Darley was a Lieutenant in the United States Marines. Mr. and Mrs. Darley must have been

2

a staid married couple when the boy who was to become the well-known illustrator was born to them. The birthplace was Philadelphia, the City of Brotherly Love, another omen of good fortune for this child.

The mother and father must have set an artistic example to their family, for one of the older children became a music teacher, and another a portrait painter. In the early days doing portraits was about the only way an artist could make any sort of a living in this new country, not quite ready yet for art in its grander forms.

After some schooling, young Darley, at the age of fourteen, was placed as an apprentice in a mercantile house. This was in 1836. But the boy had notions beyond trade and business. He liked to draw, and he put fun into his pictures. That was his escape from a hum-drum, everyday life. Some of his sketches were shown to Thomas Dunn English. This man, a writer, and a native of Philadelphia, was born in 1819 and lived until 1902. Most of his works are now forgotten, that is all but one—the ballad of Ben Bolt, set to music by Nelson Kneass, in 1840. It was in 1842 when he first discovered Darley's drawings, and feeling quite famous with his popular songs, he wanted to help others, and so, evidently through his influence, the editors of the Saturday Museum published them. And that was the beginning of a career. Before long some more of Darley's work appeared in Godey's Magazine, and in other magazines.

Godey's Lady's Book was published by Louis Antoine Godey, (1804-1878). Godey and his famed editor, Sarah Josepha Hale, built up a circulation of 150,000 subscriptions for the magazine. The best and most favored artists sought to illustrate this magazine. A woman's magazine, yes, and ridiculed by some as "cambric tea," but with most of the best writers and artists contributing to it.

This remarkable woman, Sarah Josepha Hale, lived to

3

ninety-one, working up to her ninetieth year, interested in every phase of life. And although she never traveled, and seldom left her office, she had friends and contributors all over the world. A handsome, self-reliant woman, she never wore glasses. She suffered one time from a cataract but that cleared itself up. She made her own hand lotion and a wrinkle eradicator out of brown paper and apple vinegar. One of her minor accomplishments was to revive Thanksgiving Day as a National holiday. Invalided in her early married days, she seeingly recovered her health on a diet of grapes. Thereafter she was never without this delicious fruit, and always kept a plate of grapes on her desk. Like the old Greeks and Romans, she believed the grape a gift of the gods for the wine made from it could induce such exhilaration. But Sarah Hale took her grapes straight.

In the book, "The Lady of Godey's," Sarah Josepha Hale, by Ruth E. Finley, page 258, there is an amusing note. The author advances the idea that perhaps Mrs. Hale's interest in the stage was the reason for the first cartoon she published, "A Poet in Want of a Rhyme." This was from the album of the actor, John Howard Payne, author of "Home, Sweet Home." The artist, C. R. Leslie did the sketch. Leslie was a fine historical painter, and a member of the Royal Academy.

Louis Antoine Godey was described as something like Dickens' Pickwick in looks, and like P. T. Barnum in his ways and equally successful. He went to Philadelphia. The first issue of the Godey Book, as the magazine was called, came out in July, 1832, and it did not suspend until 1898. Mrs. Hale took over the work in 1887.

Darley kept on, largely self-taught, going step by step further up in his work. In 1845, J. T. Colon had him do a series of scenes in Indian Life in outline, etched on stone. Darley was commissioned by the Philadelphia publishers, Carey & Hart, to do the illustrations for a series called, The

Library of American Humorous Works. Rather crude, this humor, but Darley could put spirit into it with his own good taste, in The Drama in Pokerville, The Bench and Bar, of Jurytown, and other Stories, by "Everpoint."

Darley del—meaning, Darley drew it. Del from the Latin word, delineavit, meaning, he, or she, drew it. This was a term that old time limners used. Darley would also sign his pictures, Darley del. Also Darley in his early days would sign his work, Darley fecit, fecit, the Latin word for, to do or make. But later on, all he needed to sign was simply, Darley.

"Everpoint," was J. M. Fields of the St. Louis Reveille. One of these tales concerns Ole Bull, the Norwegian violinist (1810-1880) and is called, "Ole Bull in the Solitude." During a concert engagement out in Saint Louis, he rides out a stormy night to view the Prairie, and describes it as he sees it. Also, another section in this book contains, "A Quarter Race in Kentucky and Other Stories, Illustrative of Scenes, Characters, and Incidents," so goes the old-fashioned and supposedly humorous words. The editor of such was Wm. T. Porter, author of, "The Spirit of the Times," "Big Bear of Arkansas," and other tales illustrated by Darley. The different sketches originally appeared nearly all in the "New York Spirit of the Times." Darley's work here appealed to the general public, mostly men, who wanted fun and caricature in their reading in the rough days of the 1840's.

But Darley did not stop here. He wanted to try for better things, and when he had read Sylvester Judd's novel, Margaret, simply to please himself he tried to do some illustrations of this work. These drawings were not published until later when Sylvester Judd, in his quiet way, got them to the notice of the manager of the American Art Union, and were favorably received. When Darley decided to come on to New York, in 1848, when he was twenty-six years old,

5

he got the commission to illustrate Washington Irving's "Rip Van Winkle," and "The Legend of Sleepy Hollow." This was work worth while. Washington Irving himself as a young man on a trip to Italy, met Washington Allston who had gone to Rome to study art. The fascinating Allston, a few years older than Irving, took him about and showed him the wonders of fabulous Italy, and Irving entranced with the paintings and all he found there, determined to become an artist himself, instead of trying for the law he was then studying.

In the book, "Life and Letters of Washington Irving," by his nephew, Pierre Munroe Irving, Washington Irving, in Vol. I, Chap. VIII, page 130, describes Allston—"He was of a light graceful form, large blue eyes, and black silken hair—a pale expressive countenance—everything about him bespoke the man of intellect and refinement." This Washington Allston (1779-1843), an American, who painted as well as wrote, a native of South Carolina, had studied with Benjamin West at the Royal Academy in London and also in Paris and at Rome. His works are serious, generally based on Biblical or classical matter. "The Flood," and "A Spanish Girl," are at the Metropolitan Museum in New York City. His, "Dead Men Revived," 1810, belongs to the Academy of Fine Arts, Philadelphia. Yale has "The Prophet Jeremiah." He also made portraits of West and of Samuel Taylor Coleridge. So, when Washington Irving met this gifted one in the heyday of his youth, it is small wonder that he, too, yearned to devote himself to art. But good sense triumphed over desire and he went forward to a famous career of his own, in the writing field.

Irving was born in 1783, in New York City. Although two brothers attended Columbia College, Washington Irving did not seem meant for college courses, and at sixteen entered a law office, but spent most of his time in reading and wandering along the Hudson River bank, all of which he turned to good account later on. He was one of the first American authors to be recognized abroad. His "Rip Van Winkle," and the "Legend of Sleepy Hollow" are believed known to almost everyone, certainly to most Americans. He felt Darley was just the one to illustrate his quaint, satiric yet humorous tales. Later in his life, he said to his nephew, Pierre Irving, in talking about artists in general and Darley in particular, "Jarvis tried but failed to embody my conception of Diedrich Knickerbocker; Leslie also. Darley hit it in the Illustrated History of New York. My idea was that he should carry the air of one profoundly impressed with the truth of his own history," This quotation is from, "Life and Letters of Washington Irving," by his nephew, Pierre Irving, Vol. IV, Chap. XV, pages 242, 243.

Washington Irving died at his beloved Sunnyside, in 1859, leaving behind him happy memories and some immortal characters, such as, Rip Van Winkle, and the schoolmaster, Ichabod Crane. Note his Sketch Book in the well-known format, put out in 1854, by G. P. Putnam and Company, then at 10 Park Place. This book was illustrated by Darley, making an excellent combination of author and artist and publisher.

There is the Rip that everyone knows waking from his long sleep, a symbolic story. Many a one drowses on, day after day, in a rut of life, and then somehow jogged awake, finds the world a place of daze, all changed, everything has passed him by. And Ichabod Crane, yes, Darley hit it right there, too—the long nose, the satisfied expression, the simplicity of the man who, with his assumption of wisdom, tried to put it over on others. But he was eventually shown up for what he was.

Yes, Irving and Darley and Putnam, hit it there. The very name, Putnam has a deal of history connected with it. There was Israel Putnam, the old Revolutionary soldier, born in 1718, and living until 1790. In 1778 he made his noteworthy escape from the British troops under Tryon, by riding down the stone steps at Horseneck. He had a cousin, Rufus, living from 1738 to 1824, also a Revolutionary War soldier. Then there was Mary Putnam, (1810 to 1898), who was a sister of the poet, James Russell Lowell, one famous family marrying into another. Then George Palmer Putnam (1814-72), the American publisher. In 1848 he established his own publishing business. We are told he was a friend of his authors and they were plenty—Poe, Irving, Cooper, Bryant, Carlyle, Lowell, Bayard Taylor, and George Curtis who helped establish Putnam's Magazine. Putnam was also a founder and an honorary member of the Metropolitan Museum of New York City. George Haven Putnam (1844-1930), was born in London, and became an author and publisher. He was a member of the G. P. Putnam Co. in 1862, and then became its head in 1872. He was active in the adoption of the International Copyright Law in 1891.

The artist Jarvis referred to a while back by Washington Irving in speaking to his nephew, Pierre, was described by Verplanck, the essayist, as a man "with a Punch-like form and visage, the unidealized and unrefined Reynolds of his time and country, with a penchant for odd practical jokes, and a dependence on the bottle." A cruel description.

Dunlop wrote a diography of this Jarvis. This William Dunlop (1766-1839) was born in Perth Amboy, New Jersey and died in New York. In 1784 he went to London where he worked under Benjamin West. He was very active and interested in art, theatre, and literature, and wrote a history of art.

Jarvis made full-sized portraits of all the military and naval officials, and these are now in the City Hall, New York City. Robert Leslie (1794-1859) was born in England, but was of American parentage. He became a member of the Royal Academy. He lived mostly in England and died there.

8

And so though both these artists, Jarvis and Leslie, tried to please Irving, he chose wisely Felix Octavius Carr Darley to illustrate his work.

Oliver W. Larkin's book, Samuel F. B. Morse, And American Democratic Art, edited by Oscar Handlein, published by Little Brown and Company, Boston, Toronto, 1954, has an editorial preface signed by Oscar Handlein. This preface holds that though the United States was heir to all the European arts, it was hard to develop them here as conditions were so different. He reminds us that in Europe the leisure class had always fostered the arts. In this country there was no such class. It was all new here, an independent country. The people here believed we should have our own ideas of literature and art. Our art and literature must teach us and enlighten us as to the ideals that set up this country's government. It must do more than serve and adorn. It must enlighten.

Samuel F. B. Morse—he, too, had four names—Samuel Finley Breese Morse, (1791-1872) was both an inventor and an artist. He invented the electric telegraph, and made up the Morse code. In the book written by his son, Edward Lind Morse, in 1914, he gives Prime's anecdote about Benjamin West (1732-1820). West was born in Springfield, Pennsylvania. He went to Europe and settled in London. His fame grew so that he was made the president of the Royal Academy. He was a very kind man, well liked by all, and especially helpful with American artists who went abroad and sought his aid. The story is told that one day Morse called on West in London at his studio. West was seated before a large painting of King George III, copying it on canvas. He asked Morse if he knew who the subject of the portrait was. And Morse said he knew it was the King. West then told him that the King was sitting for this portrait in the palace when an aide entered the room and handed His Majesty a box containing the Declaration of Independence of America. Morse wanted to know how this was received by the King. And West told Morse that the King answered, "Well, if they can find happiness in the way they have chosen, I shall be happy." Quite a different George III than the tyrant we have thought him!

Benjamin West was always loyal to the land of his birth although he lived abroad and found good fortune there. In this same book, Larkin's on Morse is this anecdote, too. While abroad Morse met Samuel Taylor Coleridge in London, and became friends, often traveling together. On one occasion Morse had with him a copy of Irving's "Knickerbocker History of New York" (illustrated by Darley) and when Coleridge asked what the book was, Morse told him it was just a book by an American. Coleridge begged to read it, and Morse handed it over, and then, as it was getting late, went to his own room in the place they were staying on their travels. The next morning he saw the light still burning in Coleridge's room, and when Morse went to the room, found Coleridge still reading the book. Morse wanted to know if he had been up all night reading it. Coleridge was surprised, "Is it late?" he said, and, then, "Who is the author?" Later Irving and Coleridge met and became warm friends. No wonder the book and its illustrations charmed him.

This same Coleridge had a strong leaning toward American ideals. Samuel Coleridge wrote: "The Rime of the Ancient Mariner" and "Kubla Khan" and much else. He was born in 1772—1834 he died. Coleridge and Robert Southey (1774-1843) another English poet ("The Battle of Blenheim," and "The Inchcape Rock") dreamed of founding an utopia, a Pantisocracy, on the banks of the Susquehanna River in the United States. But lack of money ruined this fine idea.

Washington Irving and Darley were among those who helped make New York famous. Knickerbocker was an old

10

Dutch family name, and now, because of Irving's history, has become the name for all the early Dutch settlers here, taking them as a group. Sleepy Hollow and Tarrytown were immortalized by him, Sleepy Hollow, the place of placid folk, and Tarrytown where the men would linger at the tavern instead of coming straight home to supper and angry wives. John Andre, the young English spy was captured hereabouts. An American visiting London many years later was quite surprised to find the British regarded Andre as a hero. But this American was more wroth when he came across a statue erected in honor of Lord Cornwallis. "A whole lot of praise on the monument for Cornwallis," the American fumed, "and not a word about him handing his sword at Yorktown Heights to General Washington!" But Cornwallis was ill that fateful day, and General O'Hara had to take his place.

Many of the foremost writers of all nations wrote and published critiques of Cooper's works. Balzac stands out with his article on Cooper's novel, "The Pathfinder"—"Fenimore Cooper et Walter Scott," (Oeuvres completes, Vol. XXIII) translated by Katherine Prescott Wormsley in The Personal Opinions of Honore de Balzac, 1908, and his conversation about Cooper (Balzac en Pantoufles, by Leon Goslan, 1856), translated, "Balzac in Slippers."

Edgar Allan Poe gave an adverse criticism of Cooper's novel, "Wyandotte," in Graham's Magazine, Nov. 1843, reproduced in the Stedman-Woodberry edition. Herman Melville offered a criticism of Cooper's, "Story of The Sea Lions," in the Literary World, April 28, 1849. And Mark Twain wrote a humorously devastating review, called, "Fenimore Cooper's Literary Offenses." Further along more will be told about this essay. This piece by Mark Twain appeared in the North American Review, July, 1895.

But both Cooper and Darley have withstood good and bad criticism, and will continue to do so, as is the case with everything worthwhile. Susan Fenimore Cooper (1813-1894), an author of standing in her own right, was born at Scarsdale, New York. In the later years of his life she served as her father's secretary. Afterwards she lived at Cooperstown, developing a home for orphan girls. Miss Cooper made up an Anthology of poetry, and in a preface gives her ideas about this subject. She refutes the old notion that poetry came first in a nation or country, and that prose developed later. To her way of thinking poetry is the final achievement of a civilization, its golden age, just before it starts to go downhill.

Quite true art matters were in a poor way here in America in the early days of the United States. It is on record that at the first international exhibit held here in New York, busts were shown of Washington and Henry Clay made in white soap. Another atrocious showing was a figure of the Saviour modelled in butter. Like Darley, many of our artists were self-taught, but all did not have his genius.

Charles Bulfinch (1763-1844) was the first professional architect here. He designed the Boston State House (1799), the University Hall at Harvard (1815), the Massachusetts General Hospital (1820), and he worked on the Capitol at Washington, from 1810 to 1830.

In her book, Art in America, Susan LaFolette, Harper & Brother publishers, New York and London, on page 66, gives the idea that art was not looked upon as a profession of much worth by the older people, and she gives an anecdote about John Trumbull (1756-1843), who later became a famous historical painter after studying under Benjamin West, and whose "Declaration of Independence" is in the Capitol at Washington. As a young aspirant, Trumbull was trying to get his father's consent to adopting art as a calling. Young Trumbull spoke to him of the fame attached to artists and the honor and awards given them in Athens. But his father, Governor Jonathan Trumbull of Connecticut

12

(1710-1785), cut him short with the words, "Connecticut is not Athens."

Further on in the LaFolette book, pages 122-123, we read how the increasing number of illustrated books and magazines offered work to painters and engravers. Such works are mentioned as,—Herring and Longacre's National Portrait Gallery, Harper's Family Bible, or the illustrated sets of gift books, and such magazines as Godey's Lady's Book, and later Harper's Weekly. Harper's Weekly sent Winslow Homer as Special Correspondent to the Civil War front, to write and to sketch. And we read in this book that some of the foremost artists were illustrators, and one of these illustrators was of the foremost artists, Darley. And this book goes on to say that, "the work of F. O. C. Darley was not as definitely outmoded as most of the contemporary painting." The admission is made that there is sometimes a little sentimentality in his work, saying, "It would be hard to illustrate such an author as Cooper unsentimentally." And the book goes on to say the quality of Darley's drawing saved it from banality. We are told further there was no taint of the amateur "in his work in its swift, sure, expressive lines."

On page 172 of this interesting book, "Art in America," are the words, "It is not in the English temperament to express itself graphically, its natural expression is literary." The bland southern skies demand pictures. The cold northern worlds use words to express everything—Shakespeare for England; Michelangelo for Italy.

Darley was born in the time of the James Monroe administration, in 1822, and he lived through the administrations of Monroe, John Quincy Adams; Andrew Jackson; Martin Van Buren; William Henry Harrison; John Tyler; James K. Polk; Zachary Taylor; Millard Fillmore; Franklin Pierce; James Buchanan; Abraham Lincoln; Andrew Johnson; Ulysses S. Grant; Rutherford B. Hayes; James Garfield;

Chester Arthur; and Grover Cleveland was in office when Darley died in 1888.

He had been through the years under eighteen Presidents, in the sixty-six years he lived. This span was a formative period for the nation. Monroe's office term was called, The Era of Good Feeling. John Quincy Adams was much against slavery and promoted the Smithsonian Institution. Andrew Jackson, a military hero, was all for the good of the little man. William Henry Harrison opened up Ohio and Indiana to settlers. John Tyler was the first Vice-President to succeed a President. Millard Fillmore approved the Treaty that opened up Japan to Western commerce. Franklin Pierce was well-meaning but mediocre. James Buchanan tried hard for peace. Abraham Lincoln was the Great Emancipator. Andrew Johnson purchased Alaska. U. S. Grant won the War. Rutherford Hayes proved a conservative. Garfield was assassinated. Arthur gave a dignified and honorable administration. Grover Cleveland proved to be both a reformer and a conservative. Grant was in as President at the time of the Centennial in Philadelphia, in 1876. Darley in his quiet way went on to success through these developing years.

In the book, The History of the Ideals of American Art, by Eugene Neuhaus (Professor of Arts at the University of California, 1931,) declares, page 414, "many artists were illustrators exclusively. One of these, wedded to the field by special gifts, was Felix O. C. Darley." And, further, "Darley's industry was as great as his facility. The free swing of his style and the sense of reality and action gave his work distinction."

A while back we quoted that the graphic arts were for the Southlands, and the literary arts for the North. But exception can be taken to that when we speak of the United States. This golden continent of North America is not like the bleak northern parts of Europe. Here we have every kind of climate and weather, North, South, East, West. In

14

time we should excel graphically as well as in a literary way. It is easier to write and talk indoors in cold climate. In the warm, sunny lands, nature with abundant gifts calls one outdoors to enjoy the sights and to express them in song and picture.

Philip Hone (1780 to 1851) was one time Mayor of New York, and his diary is of great historic interest. Speaking of Morse, the artist and inventor, Hone remarked that although Morse had been to Italy, the skies there had not warmed him. Hone conceded that Morse was well-versed in all the principles of art, but there was, "no poetry about his painting," and moreover, "his prose consists of straight lines that look as if they had been stretched to the utmost tension, to form a clothesline." But there was nothing cold or stiff about Darley. His ideas and consequently his drawings came straight from the heart, and were natural.

Again to refer to the LaFolette book, page 86, mention is made here to what Leslie, the artist, had to say about Gilbert Stuart (1755-1828), an eminent American portrait painter, "that his pictures sometime looked as if one could blow them away." And this stricture applies to many of "these pretty portraits." And here is another invaluable bit from this same book, page 50,—This is about John Singleton Copley (1738-1815), one of America's good early portrait painters who went on to London and much honor there, but strange to say, his best art seems to have been accomplished in his earlier years in America. And this is what we read—that one reason for Copley's slow tempo was told to Dunlop by the painter, C. R. Leslie, who said that when Copley was doing a portrait, he would make with his palette knife a tint for every part of the face, whether in light, shadow, or reflection. This took him so long, even before he commenced on the canvas.

Asher Durand, another early one among American painters was born in Jefferson, New Jersey, 1796, and lived until

1886 in South Orange, New Jersey. His father was an engraver, and he took his first lessons from him. Later he turned to painting landscapes in oil and also portraits. In 1825 he was one of the founders of the National Academy of Design, and served as president of that organization from 1845 to 1861.

RIP VAN WINKLE AWAKING

(from the *Sketch Book*)

CHAPTER II

The Pride of Pulse

THE DRAWINGS that the young Darley had done to please himself so quietly, illustrating Sylvester Judd's "Margaret," launched him on his way to fame. This Sylvester Judd was an American writer (1813-1853). His first work, the novel, "Margaret," A Tale of the Real and the Ideal, was an imaginative piece of writing that appealed to Darley. Judd was an advocate of temperance, anti-slavery, and other reform movements. There is no record that Darley ever tinkered blatantly with any reforms, but his excellent, thoughtful work must have had a good influence on the world that knew him. The thirty Compositions in Outline from Judd's "Margaret," etched on stone, were published in 1856. This work was very favorably received by the public, and he was compared to the eminent German, Moritz Retzsch, considered a master of outline. It was said that Darley matched the German artist in grace, but outdid this one in the vividness of characterization.

Darley moved on to New York. In the early 1850's he illustrated Ik Marvel's "Lorgnettes." Ik Marvel was the pen name of the writer, Donald Grant Mitchell (1822-1908). His writings are whimsical, charming, and a bit sentimental. Among his popular works were—"The Reveries of a Bachelor," his most popular; "The Seven Stories with Basement and Attic"; "American Lands and Letters"; etc. He was in Paris while the 3rd French Revolution was going on, 1848, and he described this in his, "Battle Summer" (1849). Later,

17

when he was again in New York, he put out, in two volumes, "The Lorgnettes," or Studies of the Town by an Opera Goer (1850), illustrated by F. O. C. Darley.

In 1852, Darley made the title page of the comic magazine, The Lantern. He must have felt he was appreciated when chosen to illustrate James Fenimore Cooper's works for James Gregory. The Cooper illustrations, reproduced on steel by bank note engravings were also published as the Cooper Vignettes (1862) in a large volume of India paper proofs. James Fenimore Cooper was born September 15, 1789, in Burlington, New Jersey. In 1790 his father moved the family to Otsego Lake, New York. There he founded the village of Cooperstown on a tract of land, and in 1799 erected the family home there, known as Otsego Hall. Later on from hereabouts, James Fenimore Cooper gathered his knowledge of frontier life and Indian character he was to portray so well in his Leatherstocking Tales. He attended Yale, and later went to sea on a merchant ship, expecting eventually to enter the U.S. Navy. But this never happened. Cooper's first novel, "Precaution," 1820, was not well received, but the "Spy," published the next year met with such a welcome that the author decided on a literary career. "Prairie," 1827, the earliest of the Leatherstocking series. "The Last of the Mohicans," 1826, is considered by many the best of Cooper's writings." "The Pilot," 1823-1824, was the first to bring him fame. He continued writing novels until his death at Cooperstown, in 1851.

One of Cooper's stories, "The Chainbearer or The Littlepage Manuscripts," illustrated by Darley from his drawings, was published in New York, 1860, by W. A. Townsend & Company. Here is a bit of philosophy from the above story, page 23—"The Muse of History is the most ambitious of the whole sisterhood, and never thinks she has done her duty unless all she says and records is said and recorded with an air of profound philosophy, whereas, more than half of the greatest events which affect human interest are to be referred to causes that have little connection with our boasted intelligence, in any shape. Men feel more than they reason, and a litle feeling is very apt to upset a great deal of philosophy."

In another of Cooper's Stories, "Heidenmauer, or the Benedictine" illustrated by Darley, the author in the introduction, likens the Rhine to the Hudson River: "The Rhine, while it frequently possesses more of any particular species of scenery within a given number of miles than the Hudson, has none of so great excellence. It wants variety, the noble beauty and the broad grandeur of the American stream. In islands, too, the advantage is with the Hudson."

"The Monikins," by J. Fenimore Cooper, illustrated from drawings by F. O. C. Darley, New York, 1862—W. A. Townsend & Company, is a curious story, and proved not very popular. A colony of super-monkeys are found in some mystical place, presumably near the South Pole region. They have a language that the men discoverers get to understand. This language is a compound of old classical languages. These monkeys are an advanced stage of humanity, in their own opinion. It is all satire of a true but gentle sort and has some humor to it—as the monkeys have their intellect in their tails making it so much easier to estimate the greatness of the mind,—the longer the tail, the more brains therein. And so on in this comic vein, a little tiresome, and the ending not too good. It was not the success of most of Cooper's other tales.

Cooper wrote on Historical matters, and one of his books is a good but an argumentative history of the United States Navy. Cooper is quoted as saying that a country in the decline was often more enjoyable than one on the advance. Probably such a country would be still blandly enjoying its golden age, and never realizing that the luster was dimming. Cooper had a large and devoted family and they liked being together. Susan never married but devoted herself to keeping her father's memory green. Cooper was happily married. So strong was the bond between husband and wife, they never needed any demonstration to prove it. If Cooper had to go on a business trip, before leaving home, he would read with his wife the prayer in the marriage service. At the end of his life, when the doctor warned that death was near, Mrs. Cooper came alone into the sick room and read this prayer to her husband. He died peacefully a few hours later. After Cooper's death a Memorial was held, and all the prominent men of the day were on hand for it, to speak of his genius.

Speaking of Cooper, at this Memorial, William Cullen Bryant said his character was like the bark of the cinnamon, "a rough and astringent rind without, and an intense sweetness within."

Darley did fine work in these illustrations for Cooper. To speak just of one of these books, and one not so well known—"The Sea Lions"—here the frontispiece, by Darley, shows the rescue party going into the cabin of the wrecked vessel in the ghastly South Pole region.—"One man there in the cabin sat leaning against a transom. His eyes were open and glared on the party around the caboose. The lips were slightly parted, and, at first, Roswell expected to hear him speak. The immovable features, rigid muscles, and wild expression of the eyeballs however soon told him the melancholy truth. The man was dead. The current of life had actually frozen at his heart."

Professor Dixon Ryan Fox, in "Decline of Aristocracy," p. 22, describes Cooper's father as, "the mirror of perfection as a Federalist Squire." Cooper's "Pioneers," gives a picture of his early life, (and pretty soft it was). In the book, "Fenimore Cooper, Critic of His Times," by Robert Ernest Spiller, New York, 1931, this anecdote is given, p. 242, a repeat from the Rev. Ralph Birdsall's, "Story of Cooperstown," pages 245-247—A Miss Williams, who lived on Main Street, and who had known Cooper as a boy, used to call out to him as he passed by, "James, why don't you stop writing those silly novels, and make something of yourself?"

"The Water-Witch," illustrated by Darley, is considered Cooper's most imaginative piece of work. Here is a sample of it—"As if never wearied with her kindness, Nature has placed the island of Manhattan at the precise point that is most desirable for the position of a town."

The Oak Openings, or The Bee-Hunter," by J. Fenimore Cooper, with illustrations from drawings by F. O. C. Darley, New York, 1860, W. A. Townsend and Company, opens with a description of Michigan as a wild region. "Although wooded, it was not as the American forest is wont to grow, with tall straight trees towering toward the light, but with intervals between the low oaks that were scattered profusely over the view and with much of the air of negligence that one is apt to see in grounds where art is made to assume the character of nature. The trees, with very few exceptions, were what is called the "burr-oak," a small variety of a very extensive genus. And the spaces between them, always irregular and often of singular beauty, have obtained this name of "openings,"—the two terms combined giving their appellation to the particular species of native forest under the name of "Oak Openings." Anyone writing in this far-seeing, detailed fashion would want Darley to illustrate his work. In the Oak Openings of Cooper, p.27, we read that the word, shanty, may be a corruption of "chiente," thought to be French-Canadian for "dog Kennel." "Chiente," is the right word for such. On page 28, "Yankee," is a slight corruption of the word, "yengese a term applied to the English by the Indians. Also, "Castle Meal," was a corruption of "chateau au miel."

It would seem that Darley brought good fortune to the writers whose work he illustrated. He "illuminated" them, brightened and filled the texts with light, and normal and happy and often comic life. It seems true that both Irving's and Cooper's best writings when linked with Darley's drawings, interested more readers than when Darley was absent from their pages.

Things were going well with Darley. He was making money, getting to be famous. So he married in 1859, at the mature age of thirty-seven, but one can be sure that he was still youthful, growing in mental stature, developing his idea of art in his quiet, sensitive way. His bride had a sensible name, Jane, and she was the daughter of Warren Colburn, the arithmetician, a fine family with which to be connected —mathematics are connected with logic and philosophy, just what an artist needs for a balance, a sort of golden mean. After he was married, he established his home in Claymont, in the State of Delaware one of the original thirteen States and the first to ratify the United States Constitution, December 7, 1787. Delaware is called the Diamond State. This is a wholesome, healthy region with the Delaware Bay and the Delaware River, and Delaware Water Gap, an ideal home spot for an artist, and not too far away from the great busy city, New York City. So Darley continued on and upward in his famous career. He was a very busy man. He kept on drawing for Appleton's and Harper's. Daniel Appleton, the American publisher and the founder of a large printing house under the name of D. Appleton & Co., was born in Haverhill, Massachusetts in 1785. His son, who lived from 1814 to 1899, was associated with him and he began to publish books on his own account in 1831. This son became a partner in 1838. The name Appleton is an honored one in this country. There was a Samuel Appleton away back in 1766-1853, a merchant and a philanthropist. Then Nathan Appleton, 1779-1861, introduced the use of the power-loom into the United States for the manufacture of cotton cloth.

Thomas Gold Appleton, 1812-1884, was an author and a wit. Susan Hale edited his Life and Letters.

Harper & Brothers, New York Printing and Publishing firm, had its beginning in 1817, as J. & J. Harper, two brothers, James (1795-1869), and John (1797-1875). They were a farmer's sons, Joseph Harper of Newtown, Long Island. In 1825 two other brothers, Joseph Wesley (1801-1870) and Fletcher (1806-1877) were admitted to the firm. This important firm had issued around two hundred works before the firm name was changed in 1833 to, Harper & Brothers. They put out Harper's Magazine, founded in 1850, and Harper's Weekly, also in the Fifties, and the fashion magazine, Harper's Bazaar in 1867. It was Harper's Weekly that sent Winslow Homer as Special Correspondent and Artist to the Civil War front. Winslow Homer (1836-1910), was very popular as an illustrator, and well known for his water colors of the sea. He was born in Boston. He studied lithography for two years. After a while in New York, he finally setled in Maine. He had traveled in Europe, and had successful exhibits in Paris, Brussels and Antwerp. His best known works are his landscapes and his marines.

Besides doing illustrations for the aforesaid publishers, Darley did many other illustrations. There were the Christmas Stories by Edward Everett Hale, "Christmas Eve," and "Christmas Day." Edward Everett Hale was born the same year as was Darley, 1822, but outlived him by twenty-one years, dying in 1909. Perhaps he is best known for his tale, "The Man Without a Country" (1863), also, "In His Steps," (1873); "A New England Boyhood." His collected works were published in 1901. As a clergyman, he was famous as a preacher. He edited, "Lend a Hand," and contributed to many periodicals. He was very active in philanthropic endeavors. His, "Ten Times One Is Ten," (1870), started a number of clubs, and other benevolent organizations. He founded and edited The Christian Examiner, and also Old and New, which finally merged into Scribner's Monthly. For the last six years of his life he was Chaplain of the United States Senate. His sister, Lucretia Peabody Hale wrote children's stories—"The Peterkin Papers."

Hale is another famous name in American Annals. There was Nathan Hale (1755-1776), the patriot of the American Revolutionary War. In September, 1776, he volunteered to enter the British lines to get some information for General Washington. Disguised as a schoolteacher, he reached Long Island where he was caught and condemned to death as a spy. The picture that Darley drew to illustrate this sad event is in this book. We see here the defiant young man facing his fate with the time-honored words (sometimes debated), "My only regret is that I have but one life to lose for my country!" and we read on the picture, "Stung by this reply, the infuriated officer exclaimed, 'Swing the rebel up!' And in a moment more, the spirit of Nathan Hale had passed away, a noble sacrifice in American liberty." We are told further that this tragedy happened in early autumn, 1776. It is said that the enemy destroyed Hale's letters to his friends, for the Provost-Marshall declared, "So that the rebels might not know they had a man who could die with such firmness."

In this drawing by Darley of Nathan Hale, the group of curious and sympathetic women, gathered nearby, show their horror on their faces. A child clings, terrified, to its mother's skirts. Another woman holds her babe on high to attest how dear freedom is. The engraver of Darley's drawing was A. H. Ritchie. The title of the book in which this picture appeared was, "The Adventures and Achievements of Americans." This scene is placed at the Beekman house, 51st Street near First Avenue, New York City.

Darley also did drawings for large framing prints, much in demand. Among these, one, styled, "On the March to the Sea," was Darley's best known. This picture was also done with A. H. Ritchie. Another opening for Darley's works were the fine vignettes for bank notes. The definition of vignette, in Webster's Dictionary, indicates it is from the French, meaning a vine—l. Orig.—a running ornament of vine leaves, tendrils, etc. as used in decoration. 2, Hence now—(a) a small decoration, design or illustration of any kind put on, or just before, the title page, at the beginning or end of a chapter, etc. of a manuscript or book. (b) Hence, as such pictures are often without a definite bounding line, any picture, as an engraving, photograph, or the like, which shades off gradually into the surrounding ground, or the unprinted paper. 3. In general, a picture, illustration, or depiction in words, especially one of small or dainty kind.

Another picture that Darley did was titled, "George Washington's Triumphal Entry into New York, 1783." Here is a tremendous throng so well adjusted by the careful artist that characters stand out—the frightened children running from the horses' hoofs as the soldier rider tries to keep the path clear and all out of danger. Then there is that arrogant man out front with the soldier on horseback shaking his finger at him. The scene throbs with the life and excitement of this great day. The group safely up on the balcony wave white handkerchiefs. And then, the majestic figure comes riding along—the one, the only Washington.

The Alexander Hay Ritchie who did these pictures for Darley was born, Jan. 14, 1822, the same year as Darley, but lived longer, until Sept. 19, 1895. Besides being an engraver, he was also a painter of importance. Born in Glasgow, he studied drawing with the distinguished painter, Sir William Allan. In 1841 Ritchie came to this country, working for a while in Canada, and then settling in New York. In 1847, he set up for himself in his own engraving establishment, and was so successful he had to hire assistants. That was a great time for engravings. Every home had them on the walls. Ritchie was very particular and conscientious, and it used to be said, that he put the finishing touches on every plate that came through his shop. He was especially good in engraving in mezzotints, some of them of his own paintings. He exhibited his oils at the National Academy. His first appearance there was in 1848. He also did portraits—Dr. James McCosh, president of Princeton, and Prefessors Alexander and Hodge of the Princeton faculty. He made difficult group pictures, like the Class of 1863, Yale College, with forty-eight members in the picture. He also did, "The Authors of the U.S." after the original of Thomas Hicks.

This Thomas Hicks was of Quaker ancestry, born in Newton, Bucks County, Pennsylvania, in 1823. He began as a boy to try to paint. He did a portrait when he was only fifteen years old. He studied in Philadelphia, and then at the National Academy in New York, and also at Rome and Paris. His portraits were highly popular. How fortunate for Darley to be associated with Ritchie, but Darley seemed fortunate in many ways. His family was related to the portrait painter, Thomas Sully. There must be something in heredity. Thomas Sully was born in Horncastle, Lincolnshire, England, June, 1783. His parents were actors, and they brought him to America with them in 1792. Later he studied art in Charleston, South Carolina, and by 1813, he was doing very well as a portrait painter in Richmond, Virginia. He then came on to New York, and finally to Philadelphia. He suffered every kind of privation, and yet he kept on to an illustrious career. He loved beauty. It is said that he never painted a disagreeable picture. With actors and artists in his background, Darley too had something in his favor besides his own gifts. Sully loved music and the theatre, and as reported, suffered gallantly, "the many caprices of fortune." Sully died in 1872.

Henry T. Tuckerman, in his Book of the Arts, New York, G. P. Putnam & Son—1867—page 473 writes about Darley, "he had an intimate claim to find substance and satisfaction

26

in rendering the comedy of life into artistic significance."
And Tuckerman goes on to say that Darley possessed two
endownments—"facile power, and an original and vivid
sense of the humorous." On the same page, Tuckerman declared that the outline illustrations that Darley made for
Irving's Legend of Sleepy Hollow, "when published, formed
an epoch in our art history." Not only in this country but
abroad was his art recognized. A very advantageous offer
came from London to Darley, but home meant too much
to him to accept any work that would keep him long away.
Darley's illustrations of Dickens' works were enthusiastically
received. And Tuckerman in the book quoted above, page
474, writes of Darley's expressive depiction of a scene from
the Pickwick Papers—the visit of the Rev. Mr. Stiggins to
the incorrigible Sam Weller in Prison. Here old Tony leans
upon the back of an arm chair enjoying Sam's mock solici-
tude for the physical welfare of "the Shepherd," while Mrs.
Weller is sentimental in another corner of the room.

Tuckerman says that Darley's designs for Cooper's novels
were five hundred in number. Large copies of some of the
best were separately published. The Prince Napoleon, on a
yachting trip to this country, commissioned Darley to do four
scenes for his private collection:—"Emigrants Attacked by
Indians on the Prairie"—"The Unwilling Laborer"—"The
Repose"—and "The Village Blacksmith."

During the Civil War Darley dramatized, with his vivid
pencil, many of the scenes. One of these pictures was, "A
rebel woman handing a cup of water to a tired, dusty Union
soldier." Tuckerman, on page 475, says that Darley had, "An
equal facility in true, literal transcript, and in fanciful
conception."

In his book, "The History of Ideals of American Art,"
Eugene Neuhaus, Prof. of Art, University of California,
1931, explains that a print is not something merely mechanical, but a free forceful highly personal medium of ex-

pression." "More and more artists, year by year, are drawn to its practice." He goes further, saying that copies of drawings may be made from engraved metal plates is said to have been accidental and relatively recent, although the printing of pictures from wood blocks with the designs on them in relief is very old and was highly perfected by the Chinese and Japanese centuries before metal engraving was practised." And Prof. Neuhaus goes on to say, "Wood engraving, for the purpose of printing from a flat wood-block on which certain parts had been cut away so as to leave others in relief in masses rather than in lines, is best studied in the prints of the Japanese masters, that caused so much enthusiasm in the second half of the last century when the Orient opened its doors to the Western world."

It is believed that metal engraving came down from the art of the goldsmith or the armorer in the 15th century when such works were engraved or ornamented with incised lines filled in with black enamel. And, it is said, that it was accidentally discovered, that a moistened paper pressed against these engraved lines covered with prepared ink, would give a copy of the engraving. Probably this was the beginning of printing. Finally it was found out that an acid—a mordant—would do the work on the metal easier and quicker than was possible with the burin. The burin is the pointed steel cutting tool, the graver.

Steel engravings were popular for a long while; then this line became commercialized. Now steel engraving is used for making banknotes, visiting cards, and stamps.

The lithograph was discovered, so Neuhaus tells in his book, in 1796, Aloys Senefelder, a German, marked down the amount of his laundry bill with a piece of soap on a polished sandstone. He saw that the parts of the stone touched by soap would take ink, but the parts of the stone without soap refused the ink. So came about the making of prints with a greasy specially prepared lithographer's pencil.

Asher Brown Durand, 1796-1886, who later became the founder of the Hudson River School, did landscape painting along the Hudson River, was born in Jefferson, New Jersey, worked in his father's watch-making shop, and learned to cut cyphers on spoons, and so went on to engraving and printing.

Robert Weir was born in New York, 1803, and lived until 1889. He became a portrait and historical painter. He was also professor of drawing at the Military Academy at West Point. When he went to Italy, in a reckless mood, he could not resist the beauty of a suit of armor. Then to atone for this extravagance, we are told he lived a month on ten cents a day. So declares Tuckerman, page 205.

Tuckerman felt there was a touch of Hogarth in Darley's works. William Hogarth (1697-1764), was the English painter and engraver. He won fame and fortune with his engravings. He was a great satirist, but Darley did not equal him in savagery, and his subjects, the people were of a later day. Hogarth was harsher, all for social reform. In his own time his paintings and normal pictures were somewhat neglected, but his "Shrimp Girl," is in the National Gallery in London. Certainly Darley could depict all sorts and conditions of men and life, but if there was ugliness to be shown up, he did it quietly but adequately. In a mood certainly far from most of Hogarth's works, were Darley's illustrations for Longfellow's works, especially "Evangeline." This picture shown here, of the Acadian Women from the neighboring hamlets and farms, is proof. The English fleet had appeared in the harbor, and all the Acadians had been summoned to meet in the church in the morning, by the command of the English King. Nothing else was divulged to this peaceful village of Grand-Pre. So the people gathered with their children as summoned. And then the bell sounded in the tower, and the drum beat over the meadow filled with men, the women waiting outside in the church-yard.

And then came the heart-rending Proclamation—"All your lands and dwellings and cattle forfeited to the Crown, and that you yourselves be transported from this province to other places!" Silent a moment they stood in speechless wonder, and then rose louder and ever louder a wail of sorrow and anger. The men were imprisoned and taken away. And here we see the women waiting to be likewise transported, families broken up, ties disrupted. Darley has caught the awful grief of the women in this picture. When would they see their loved ones again? When would they be reunited? What did life hold out for them now? The children with their pets, looking frightened but not understanding, clung to their weeping mothers.

And the second picture shown here, drawn by Darley, "When they had reached the place, they found only embers and ashes." Here is Evangeline and Basil, searching for Gabriel, find nothing but embers and ashes, and must go on again, looking . . . looking. Darley made twenty-four drawings of the pitiful scenes—all with great delicacy and spirit. Darley must have caught some of the mannerisms of his relative, the painter, Thomas Sully, depicted the women on the North American Continent as possessing a more fragile, almost angelic appearance in contrast to the sturdier women of the European countries and elsewhere on the globe. We understand that was Sully's opinion of the American women.

And often some faithful dog appears in Darley's pictures —barking in happy exultation when the master is rejoicing, or looking on with mournful eyes, somehow feeling the sadness when all around are depressed.

THE SINGING LESSON

(from *The Legend of Sleepy Hollow*)

Courtesy of Putnam's & Coward-McCann

CHAPTER III

In Good Company

DARLEY WAS ELECTED to the National Academy of Design in 1852, at the age of thirty, with a good bit of work already excellently done. And after that he became a regular exhibitor at the annual Exhibition. When Morse, the artist and inventor, settled in New York, in 1825, there then existed the American Academy of Art, and John Trumbull was the president of this institution. Trumbull was then a mature man of sixty-nine. His large picture, THE SIGNING OF THE DECLARATION OF INDEPENDENCE, is in the Capitol at Washington, D.C. Later he founded the Trumbull Gallery at Yale, 1831. But when Morse arrived in town, in all the vigor and drive of his thirty-fourth year, he found much dissatisfaction in this American Academy of Art. So, in 1826, there was organized the National Academy of Design, with Morse as its first president. In 1845 Morse was eletced again. On his first coming to New York, Morse found the artists generally at odds, and he decided to do something about this unhappy state of affairs. One evening, he invited a number of fellow artists to his rooms to partake of strawberries and cream, but in reality to get them in an agreeable mood. The strawberries and cream and whatsoever else served that night must have done the trick, for out of that meeting arose the National Academy of Design. It was decided this body was to be democratically managed by the artists themselves, by the artists, with the artists, and for the artists. It would exhibit the work of living men, and would

31

offer free instruction and prizes to art students. The four branches of art it would represent were painting, sculpture, architecture, and engraving. After its incorporation in 1825, it was characterized as standing for the traditional. But since it joined in 1906 with the Society of American Artists, it adopted a more liberal policy, now excluding only the most radical work.

Thomas Cummings, for many years Secretary and recorder of the Academy of Design, was born in England but was brought to this country in infancy. He studied with Henry Inman. Inman was born in Utica, New York, and lived until 1846. He did miniature and water colors, but his health was poor, and he did not accomplish all he wished. Cummings gives a number of anecdotes as he writes along in his records. One was the sad story of a certain architect, a man of prominence who had built the Union Bank, and St. Paul's Church in Baltimore. He met with a pitiful death, surrounded by friends but unaided by them. He was engaged in Morristown, New Jersey, superintending the completion of the interior of a church which he had designed and built. Taken suddenly ill with the cholera, then an epidemic, his frightened workmen and comrades ran away for fear of catching the dread disease. Deserted and for want of assistance, he died there in the church.

And then there is another anecdote in Cumming's Records that indicates the humanity of Darley. Louis Lang was taken sick in New York. This artist, Lang, born in 1814, and died in 1893, was a native of Waldsee, Wurtemberg, Germany. He studied at Stuttgart and at Paris, and then came to America. Darley heard he was ill and immediately went to him. The door of his room was shut, and he refused to admit anyone. Darley called out and a voice from within the room called, "Go away!" It was Lang, very sick with the smallpox. Darley kicked the door open and went in and stayed with the patient taking tender care of him. Darley

32

took the disease and had it even worse than Lang. However both men recovered, but "Darley bore the ugly marks of the pestilence to the end in honorable memory of his devotion," so the sympathetic Cummings declares in his book, "Occasional Dottings by the Wayside." Cummings was Professor of the Arts of Design in the New York University.

The National Academy of Design was another good point for Darley. It must be noted here that Morse sought the acquaintance of Louis Jacques Mande Daguerre (1789-1851) for he was experimenting along the same line. When they met they became good friends, and Daguerre was elected an Honorary Member of the National Academy of Design. Daguerre was born in Cormeilles, Normandy. In 1831, after many experiments, the daguerreotype was given to the public, and at once became a great success, the beginning of photography. With Draper, S. B. Morse was the first to introduce the daguerreotype into this country.

The National Academy of Design now has headquarters on upper Fifth Avenue. The Society was established in 1825, and incorporated in 1828. Among the founders besides Morse were Asher B. Durand and Daniel Huntington. Huntington was elected president of the National Academy of Design in 1862. He seemed especially fitted for religious painting. He was born in New York, October 14, 1816. Tuckerman said there was body and soul to this artist's work, something of Charles Lamb in him. He died in 1906. He was a member of the Hudson River group. He interpreted Bunyan's "Pilgrim's Progress," and some of Irving's "Sketch Book." He served as president of the Academy of Design not only in 1862, but also in 1869, and in 1877.

Huntington did many portraits. His painting of Van Buren is in the State Library at Albany. He admired Sir Joshua Reynold, and he does seem to follow this master in the staidness of his characters. Sir Joshua Reynolds, the notable English painter, was alive in that palmy period from

33

1723-1790. He was certainly a gifted man with a very successful social life that included the notables in all the arts. He is credited with two thousand portraits to his credit. He was the first president of the Royal Academy, no mean honor. One of his most celebrated pictures is that of the great English actress, Mrs. Siddons, as the Tragic Muse. This picture is now in the Huntington Gallery at San Marino, California. Critics say that Daniel Huntington was not always at his best, but they agree that he nearly always offered serenity and intelligence to a public needing these attributes sorely in this new and excited world where people from all quarters came to find El Dorado.

But in most artists there is a response to the spirit of art, that can rise unselfishly when called on, forgetting the fever for fame and fortune. It is told how many artists, during the Civil War and young ones, too, with all their hardships, freely made paintings, generally small ones were wanted, around eight by ten or twelve inches, to be sold for the benefit of the Sanitary Commission Fair, which corresponded to our present Red Cross. Each and every artist freely gave his work, marked, "Pro Patria." These pictures were quickly bought up. Good prices were paid for them, too, one little painting going for eight hundred dollars, all in a good cause.

Emanuel Leutze (1816-68), the German-American artist was possessed of an exuberant nature. Tuckerman calls him an adventurer in the good sense of the word, keen for adventure and exploration. He did many paintings, all dealing with great ventures in history such as: "Columbus Before Isabella"; "The Landing of the Northmen in America"; "Queen Victoria," etc., and he landed his "Westward the Star of Empire Takes its Way"; in the Capitol at Washington, and, of course, "Washington Crossing the Delaware," in the Metropolitan Museum in New York City. Critics and artists blasted the last named painting, but many have found it effective. Take it symbolically, and then you find worth in it. Tuckerman quotes an aphorism of Emerson and applies it to Leutze "There is hope in extravagance, there is none in routine."

In this vital new yorld, life was hard, or it was soft, but few were dull here. The little man here set the pace very often—he it was who smoked the cheap cigarette because he could not afford the costly cigar. And, lo, in time, cigarettes became the thing with all, high and low. The same thing with the phonograph, and the nickelodeon, all a poor man's toys, taken up and transfigured into art. The little man here wanted pictures to hang on the walls of his home, be it ever so humble. He got the chromo—short for chromolithograph. And the knowing laughed at the gaudy colors and sentimental tone. But it added warmth to drab life. A faded ineffective aging actress, with far too bright a make-up on for the illusion of youth was called by the heartless ones, a chromo.

Of course from away back in Colonial times, people here owned fine portraits made by the best artists abroad—such portrait possessors were the Byrds of Virginia, the Saltonstalls of New England, the Beekmans of New York, and their descendants still treasure these keepsakes. Few could afford such luxuries in the early days over here. There is mention made of a limner, as a painter was called, in Perth Amboy, in 1715. That he was a Scotsman is all that is told about him, and his name is not given, but if he had a studio as it has been said, there must have been some business for him here, or else he "had come a long way to starve," as Benjamin West told a raw American artist when he arrived in England to set up his easel against so many native artists. A feast or a famine it may be with any artist if taste and fashion changes in his time, no matter how successful or famed he may have been.

James Thomas Flexner, in his book, "The Pocket History of American Painting," tells how eager Europeans were to get pictures of the new world over here. And France in the

1560's sent over Jacques Le Mayne to do water color sketches for a book to be gotten out a little later. The artist, John White, was made governor of Sir Walter Raleigh's Colony in Virginia, hoping he would picture this wonderful land for those back home to see. But it was all so wild over here, that these home-sick artists could not send back pictures that really represented things here, it was so different—the scenery and the Indians. It took years to get used to the wild grandeur found here. It was frightening. We think of frontier life as something romantic, not the horror it must have been at times, the lonely strangeness, wild animals at hand and the Indians the like of which they had never seen before.

Cooper and Irving could write with fervor about frontier life although they knew it only at its best. Darley liked to draw it, too, great open places that lay across the whole country. In Tuckerman's book, "Book of the Artists, American Artist Life," 1867, G. P. Putnam & Son, is a list of American pictures in private and public Collections. In the private collection of W. T. Blodgett, Esq., New York, appear the pictures by Darley of—"Foraging Scenes in Virginia," and "Charge At Fredericksburg." And in the private collection of J. C. McGuire, is listed Darley's "Landscape with Cattle." Up to this time Darley had not done so much painting, but more drawing for illustrations. On a trip abroad he painted, "A Scene in the Streets of Rome," this became the possession of E. Bigelow, Esq., Boston, Massachusetts.

Darley's particular study had been American subjects. It was felt by publishers and authors that his illustrations could make any book a best seller as well as an important event. Tuckerman, p. 476, remarks that Darley, "Tells a story with a dash, reveals a character by a curve, and embodies an expression with two or three dots." Such was the magic use of his pencil.

The illustrations of Sylvester Judd's "Margaret," have been called the work of a genius. Some have compared these drawings with Flaxman's. John Flaxman (1755-1826) was an English artist, born at York. He did most of his work as a sculptor. He made the designs for Wedgewood pottery. While he was in Italy, from 1787 to 1794, he did outline illustrations of the works of Homer, Eschylus, and Dante. He did monuments to Nelson and Reynolds in St. Paul's Cathedral, in London. In Buckingham Palace are his noted reliefs with scriptural subjects. His work greatly influenced the younger artists of his day His Olympian Zeus, in Guerber's, "Myths of Greece and Rome," is truly god-like.

William Dunlap, who wrote Dunlap's History of the Arts of Design in the United States, 1834, was a man of many talents. An American, he lived from 1766 to 1839. He wrote and adapted plays, was a theatre manager from 1795 to 1805, and was one of the founders of the National Academy of Design, where he served as Vice-President. In 1813, he wrote "The Life of George Cooke," the actor.

A frequent exhibitor from 1848 on was William Hart, a native of Paisley, Scotland. He was brought to this country by his parents when he was nine years old, 1831. Later, reading Dunlap's History of the Arts of the United States, the artist in him awoke. One of his landscapes illustrated Bryant's poem, "Peace and Plenty," and this is considered one of his best landscapes. His brother James also became a painter here. His "Woods in Autumn," was a much admired picture. Another characteristic piece of his was, "Moonrise in the Adriondacks." William Hart served as president of the Brooklyn Academy of Design.

James Audubon is said to have been born in Louisiana, 1780. And, again, his birthplace is given as Haiti. Others declare he was the Dauphin and escaped from France at the time of the French Revolution, and was brought to America as a child. He died in New York in 1851. As a youth he went to Paris and studied art under David. Jacques Louis David, 1748-1825, was the celebrated French painter to Louis XVI.

He painted "Madame Recamier"; Andromache"; "The Oath of the Horatii," and many, many others. Audubon made paintings from his studies of birds. One of his sons became an animal painter.

And here was Darley going his keen, but quiet way, reaching upward, receiving much praise, meeting kindred spirits, enjoying his difficult work and deep thoughts. It must have meant sweet relaxation to go back to his pleasant homestead in Claymont, a place not too far from New York where he spent much time among artists like himself.

But the Civil War upset the even flow of life everywhere, the National Academy of Design, as much as any place. There was little work for the artist to do then. No one thought of art or of pictures. "Union for the Country," was the prayer of the nation. And this troubled state continued for four long years. How did the country ever get back to normal again? It took a long while. Matters were brighter in the North than down South. Up North people actually made money now that peace had come, and they wanted to spend this money in what seemed a bright new world, wholly made over, and war ended for good.

Darley could caricature; with his quick eye he would pick out some odd point in a face or figure or gait. Just a few masterly strokes and that peculiarity would appear as the chief thing in the picture—grotesque, laughable, or enlightening. There were few he made fun of however, for he was a kind-hearted man, and he could tell swiftly worth or pretense in a character. But he had the gift of exaggeration when he wanted to employ it if necessary. The word, caricature, is from the French, meaning to overload. And then there is the opposite of caricature, the penetration to the soul, stripping bare of human frailties and revealing real basic character. Here he was a master, too, and probably did more good with his sympathetic work. It takes a God-like eye to see through man's faults and show the relation to his Maker. It must have been a picturesque situation out where Darley had a farm. In this vicinity also had lived Wertmuller, the Swedish painter, celebrated for his picture of Danae of the classic myth, the mother of Perseus.

One who really went in for caricature with a vengeance was Thomas Nast (1840-1902). He was German-born and brilliant. He drew for Harper's Weekly, reporting the Civil War. He also used his sharp pen and pencil to show up evil doings in New York City. It is understood that he originated the elephant, donkey and tiger, as symbols of the Republican party, the Democratic party, and Tammany Hall. He also illustrated books. The Tweed Ring evoked Nast's scorn which he portrayed so plainly in his cartoons. William Marcy Tweed lived between 1823 and 1878. Thomas Nast helped bring about his waterloo in arousing public indignation through his drawings. Tweed suffered for his misdeeds and died in prison. The New York Times exposed Tweed's infamy.

The frontispiece in this book is a picture of Felix Octavius Carr Darley, done from an old woodcut that appeared in Harper's Weekly, 1867. He has a dedicated look—a serious face with a good nose, mouth and forehead. There is no nonsense about this picture, no vanity of dress or hair style. Here is a man of vision. There is a sense of purpose in his visage as an alert, refined American, neither too daring nor too timid, a man of the world in the best meaning of the word, with calm self-confidence unadulterated with egoism. One of our important artists declared that lack of self-confidence was almost always the cause of artistic failure, or indeed of any endeavor.

Darley could illustrate books, getting into the very mood of the author, as Washington Irving so well told his nephew. Darley also could go into the great out-doors and paint landscapes and animals and country folk. He could do almost anything with his pencil or brush, and do all things well, admirably, excellently. He was a success. His pictures sold and his services were widely sought. Flexner, in his book, "American Painting," writes that in the mid-nineteenth century Americans bought more American art than in any other time in our history. Rising national prosperity enabled many to form collections, but fortunes were not yet large enough for Americans to outbid Europeans for the master pieces of artists living or dead. Yes, Darley was thoroughly American, and therefore could amiably depict American humor and American scenes, and American character. And perhaps just because he was American and heir to all the past, he illustrated so beautifully Laurence Sterne's "Tristram Shandy." To give the book its full title, it is:—"The Life and Opinions of Tristram Shandy," "A deliberately rambling whimsical novel," that is considered one of the great works of English literature. Another of Sterne's literary offerings, almost as good as the above, is "A Sentimental Journey Through France and Italy." He started off the vogue of the sentimental novels, but few, if any of them could reach or compete with Sterne's charm. And Darley caught his exaggeration and put it down with such allurement that Laurence Sterne himself would have been pleased with it, just as Irving had been won with Darley's astuteness.

The author of Tristram Shandy, Laurence Sterne, lived from 1713 to 1768. He was British, born in Ireland in a beautiful spot, called Clonmel, that means, "The meadow of honey." In time he became an Anglican clergyman, and was stationed at Sutton, near York, and then, later, to Stillington and a prebendary's stall at York Minster. A prebend was a canon—now it is largely an honorary title in the Church of England, but in Sterne's day, probably carried a stipend. He published some sermons, but is best known for his worldly type of writings. In 1759, he wrote the first two volumes of his magnum opus, Tristram Shandy. Some other writings, too, were instantly popular, and when he went up to London, he found himself an idol. Also in 1760, he came into possession of the living of Coxwood. In 1767 he brought out more of his artful Tristram Shandy, full of the sharpest character studies in the English language. Later Sterne traveled through France and Italy getting material for his Sentimental Journey. It was the custom to dedicate books then, and so Sterne dedicated his Tristram Shandy to the Right Honorable Mr. Pitt. And the Dedication goes as follows: "Sir: Never a poor wight of a Dedicator had less hopes from his Dedication, than I have from this of mine, for it is written in a bye corner of the Kingdom and in a retired thatched home where I live in a constant endeavor to fence against the infirmities of health and other evils of life, by mirth; being firmly persuaded that every time a man smiles, but much more so when he laughs, it adds something to this fragment of life. I humbly beg, Sir, that you will honour this book, by taking it— (not under your protection—it must protect itself, but) into the country with you, where if I am ever told it has made you smile, or can conceive it has beguiled you of one moment of pain—I shall think myself as happy as a minister of State, perhaps much happier than anyone (one only excepted) that I have read or heard of I am, good Sir, your well-wisher and humble fellow subject— The Author."

William Pitt, the 1st Earl of Chatham, (1708-1778), was an English statesman. His criticism of the War of Austrian Succession brought about the downfall of Robert Walpole. On account of his denunciation of the Seven Years War he became head of the Coalition Government in1757. His policy brought about the defeat of the French in India and in Canada. Pitt broke with the Whigs over the American Colonies. He first urged conciliation, and then any settlement short of independence. In 1768, mental trouble caused him to retire. His second son, William Pitt (1769-1806) served as Prime Minister from 1783 to 1801, under George III. He established the custom of general elections. He was a liberal Tory, and advocated new taxes to cut the national debt, parliamentary reform, and reforms in India and Canada. But these reforms suffered from the French Revolution and the Wars of Napoleon. Financial support of the Allies caused a money crisis. The military coalitions against France were failures. He used bribery to further the Union with Ireland. He resigned after the King's veto of Catholic Emancipation. He was recalled in 1804, but the Austerlitz defeat was the end of his career.

The English term, Whig, is said to have come from the word, whigamore, a term applied to the Covenanters of Scotland and supposedly earlier from whiggam, a call made by drivers to urge on their horses. The word in a political sense was first used in derision. It gradually came to mean all opposed to the king. The American term, Whig, was applied to those opposing Jackson. It was a faction growing out of the Republican Party. There were many differences in the Whig Party, and by 1856, it was dissolved. The word, Tory, in England, like the term, Whig, was first a term of contempt. A Tory in politics was the opposite of a Whig. Tory was in use in England from the time of the Revolution until the Reform Bill of 1832, and then changed to the milder word, Conservative. In America, the word, Tory, was applied to anyone loyal to England and the King during the American Revolution. Webster's Dictionary declares the word, tory, is from the French, and means a pursued man, as a robber. As an epithet now it means an extreme conservatist. And so now we have gone all around through English history with the charming Tristram Shandy, and his portrayer, Felix Octavius Carr Darley who could make a name and fame for himself in any part of the globe, or any place where his art could brighten up the scene, or put life into a tale old or new.

Mathew Brady who lived from 1823 to 1896, was the

pioneer photographer in America. He made a famous photographic record of the Civil War. He also took many photographs of Lincoln, and Darley had special good likenesses done by Brady.

John Ruskin (1819-1904), in his Modern Painters, Vol. III, Part IV, Chapter 16, writes, "The greatest thing a human soul ever does in this world is to *see* something and tell what it *saw* in a plain way. Hundreds of people can talk for one who can think, but thousands can think for one who can see. To see clearly is poetry, and religion, all in one." And certainly Darley was one of the fortunate who could see and put down what he saw, so that he could make others see, too. And Homer, in the Iliad, Book XXIII declares, "It is not strength, but art, obtains the prize, And to be swift is less than to be wise." Sir Thomas Browne says, "All things are artificial, nature is the art of God." Thomas Browne (1605-1682). Whitman said that nothing can come out of an artist that is not in the man. Longfellow, "An artist never dies." Olive Schriener said, "It came to pass after a time that the artist was forgotten, but the work lived." And Santayana gives this, "An artist is a dreamer consenting to dream of the actual world." Mark Twain, in "Mark Twain at Work," tells us this—"Art is the terms of an armistice signed with faith." Walter Pater, writing about the Venetian painter who would fuse form and subordinate local color to the prevailing tone—"All art constantly aspires towards the condition of music." Pope offered this from his Essay On Criticism— "One science only will one genius fit, So vast is art, so narrow human wit." "Imagination, not invention, is the supreme master of art as of life," says Joseph Conrad, in his, "A Personal Record." And Oliver Cromwell (1509-1658) on Painting in England, with Anecdotes of Horace Walpole, offers: "Mr. Lely—I desire you would use all your skill to paint my picture like me, and not flatter me at all, but remark all these roughness, pimples, warts, and everything as you see me, otherwise I will never pay you a farthing for it." Oliver Cromwell (1599-1688), led the Puritan Revolution—the roundheads. He defeated Charles I at the Battle of Naseby. He led a cruel expedition into Ireland, and an Irishman's worst malediction is, "The curse of Cromwell on ye!"

Horace, or Horatio Walpole, the Earl of Oxford, 1717-97, was the son of the English Statesman, Robert Walpole. Horace Walpole was a literary man. He established his Strawberry Hill Press, and printed the Odes of his friend, the poet, Thomas Gray (1716-71). His most familiar work is "An Elegy Written in a Country Churchyard."

William Butler Yeats (1865-1939)—in "Two Songs from a Play," writes:- "The poet's brush consumes his dreams."

But Darley's dreams were not consumed by his brush or pencil; he kept working and dreaming on through the years, always quickened by some tale of character, and eager to portray his idea of this challenge.

William James avers that, "In art, economy is always beauty." William James, the psychologist (1842-1916) was a son of Henry James, and the brother of Henry James, the novelist and expatriated American.

Count Leo Tolstow, (1828-1910), the Russian, says in his book, "What Is Art," Chapter 8, "Art is a human activity having for its purpose the transmission to others of the highest and best feelings to which men have risen."

Whistler declared he hated anecdotal art, a picture that told a story. Darley never is anecdotal in his pictures. He gives atmosphere, mood character, and lets the viewers draw their own conclusions. Gilbert Keith Checterton (1874-1926), the English essayist, in his, "A Defence of Nonsense," gives out this, "nothing sublimely artistic has ever risen out of the pure Art, any more than anything essentially reasonable has ever risen out of pure reason. There must always be a rich moral soil for any great artistic growth."

Izaak Walton (1503-1683), the famous fisherman, declares

in "The Compleat Angler," "No man is born an artist, so no man is born an angler."

Willa Cather, the American novelist (1876-1947) in "The Song of the Lark," tells us that,—"Artistic growth is, more than it is anything else, a refining of the sense of truthfulness. The stupid believe that to be truthful is easy; only the artist, the great artist, knows how difficult it is."

In "The Gleaners," by William Wordsworth, the English poet (1770-1850), (This poem was suggested by a picture) says,

"What mortal form, what earthly face
Inspired the pencil, lines to trace,
And mingled colors, that should breed
Such rapture."

Saint Luke, the Evangelist, was born in central Syria, and it is believed he died in Beotia in A.D. 74. He studied medicine, and also art and sculpture. A painting of the Virgin Mary in St. Mary Major, at Rome is attributed to him. Early Christian art was found in the Catacombs—Bible scenes from both Testaments served to instruct the people. It has been said that art and mathematics are akin, for both try to make complicated things plain.

CHAPTER IV

Fairs and Expositions

DARLEY WAS an exhibitor at both the Paris Exposition, 1867, and in the Centennial Exposition in Philadelphia, Pennsylvania, 1876. An exposition is a public showing, an exhibition, a fair. And the word, fair, is from the French, meaning a holiday or a festival, for fairs were held on a holiday or festival time, for then people were at leisure. In the olden days, fairs were held all over Europe, and probably elsewhere, too. These fairs were special public markets, held at certain intervals, and as merchants and traders brought their wares to be sold there, fairs had better and bigger offerings than usually shown at the local markets.

Some of these fairs would last a long while, with intervals between exhibits. In the 14th Century, in France, in the Champagne country, six fairs were held at Provins, Troyes, etc., lasting through the year. As people came from all over, the money used at such fairs was a sort of international currency, hence, it is said, came the word, Troy weight.

As time went on, and people did more traveling, fairs became of less importance. One of the great old English fairs, was that of St. Bartholomew's at Smithfield, London, and this continued until 1853. We have heard of the fairs at Leipzig with their furs, and the fairs at Frankfort, and at Nigni-Novgorod, and those in Italy. The fairs in the United States were simply local entertainments largely, to exhibit cattle or garden stuff or home-made articles to be sold for charity.

46

France took the lead in holding the first big modern fair in Paris, 1798. Then came the first great International exhibit, a World's Fair in the fairyland of the Crystal Palace, at London, 1851, in Hyde Park. This marvellous building was completely made of glass, all of it except the flooring and the joists. A wonder, indeed. This building was 1851 feet long, just as the year was 1851. The cost was about $800,000, an enormous sum for those days. At the end of the year this building was removed to Sydenham, where an estate was purchased at South Kensington, where later was to be South Kensington Museum, the Royal Horticultural Society, the Albert Museum, etc.

In 1873, a great exhibition was held at Vienna, where it was said, it was visited in six months by six million people. Not to be outdone, the United States decided on a World's Fair for 1876, to celebrate the One Hundredth Year of our independence, 1776-1876. We wanted to show how we had grown as a nation in that short time, and what we had accomplished. The exposition was held in Philadelphia, naturally, as that was where the nation started, opening May 10th, 1876, and closing November 10th, 1876. Darley exhibited at this Centennial, and was well received with many tributes and praise and favorable comments. But this was not his first exhibition triumph. At the Paris Exposition of 1867, he had met with like success.

All these famous fairs led up to the Columbian Exposition, in Chicago, that started Oct. 1st, 1893, to celebrate the four hundredth anniversary of the discovery of America by Christopher Columbus, Oct. 12th, 1492, the greatest event to happen since the Birth of Christ!

The World's Fair out in Chicago was called the White City. It was hailed for its architectural achievements and its sculpture and statues shown there. On page 57, in the La-Folette book, we read, "The Centennial Exposition of 1876, in Philadelphia, impressed upon American minds that artistically all was not for the best in the best of all countries. The unavoidable comparison between foreign and American exhibits in the fine and industrial arts was all in favor of the former, the foreigners."

Darley's "Street Scene in Rome," was shown at the Centennial Exposition in Philadelphia, in 1876. And Darley's picture, "Cavalry Charge at Fredericksburg," was in the Paris Exposition of 1867.

As said here before, in the old days, when goods could not be brought quickly and easily to markets on account of poor transportation, fairs were very much in order. People from different countries could get together and exchange goods and ideas. Fairs can be traced back to Greek and Roman days. And by the Middle Ages, Fairs were in their glory, especially in the 13th and 14th centuries. Then as time went on, intercourse between people of different lands became easier, and fairs went out of existence.

The Eiffel Tower was erected for the great Paris Exposition of 1889. This tower was 984 feet high. Alexandre Gustave Eiffel (1832-1923) was a French engineer and a bridge and viaduct builder. He was born at Dijon. In 1860, he founded at Levallais-Perrit (Department Seine) an iron works. He built the renowned Garabit Viaduct over the Douro at Oporto in 1876; also the movable dome at Nice; and the framework for Bartholdi's immense Statue of Liberty, in New York harbor. The mother of Bartholdi served as the model for the Lady of the Statue. Eiffel also invented a type of movable bridge in 1885. In spite of all that good work, he was condemned, in 1893, to two years in prison and fined $4000 for breach of trust in connection with the Panama Canal works.

Eiffel erected the Tower for the Paris Exposition of 1889. It is in the Champs de Mars, and is 984 feet high, 429 feet higher than the Washington Monument. The base of the Eiffel Tower is a square, 112 yards from each corner on

GEORGE WASHINGTON'S TRIUMPHAL ENTRY INTO NEW YORK, 1783

Courtesy of The J. Clarence Davies Collection,
Museum of the City of New York

which rest the four curving supports of interlaced iron work. At the height of 590 feet, these supporters come together to form a single support. There are three platforms arranged at various heights, ascended by elevators or staircases, the latter with 1927 steps in all. The total cost of this was over a million dollars, of which the government contributed about $300,000.

In 1909 the Tower became the property of the City of Paris. In 1867 the Paris Review complained about the 1867 Paris Exposition that the paintings displayed there by the various countries were, "like brands of calico," and "they differed so little, good but not individual or characteristic enough." At this Exhibition, Darley had there his painting, "Charge at Fredericksburg, Virginia." And the Americans did not do too badly in all, as Frederick Church's "Niagara," won a prize.

The Bartholdi who did the Statue of Liberty, was the French sculptor, Frederic Auguste Bartholdi, (1834-1904), of Italian ancestry. The French government gave us his Statue of Liberty in commemoration of our independence. Bartholdi's best known works were this Statue of "Liberty Enlightening the World," and his "Lion of Belfort."

Whistler declared, "There never was an artistic period. There never was an artistic nation. "In his book, "American Artists," Royal Cortissoz says on page 315, "Probably art started late here, but when it came there was no stopping it." And, "It dated from the Centennial Exposition. Prior to that time the development of taste had been impeded by the Civil War." Cortissoz holds that in the Seventies, matters began to be better. Artists and the whole public had been aroused by what they saw at this Centennial. In the 1870's there was more money around, and the possessors of this money wanted to spend it on things of value,—they wanted to get their money's worth in art as well as in the every day things of life. Money is not the root of all evil. The want of it can break one's back with trouble's pack. It is from the *love* of money that evils shoot, money is not evil's root.

This Royal Cortissoz, was born in New York City. He became a writer and a critic, Art Editor of the New York Tribune. He edited Don Quixote, and "The Autobiography of Benvenuto Cellini." His book quoted here, "American Artists," was published in 1923.

Perhaps New York City led the way in the Renaissance of Art. Art dealers flourished, and art auctions went after the big buyers. Cortissoz tells how this new interest in art here touched many subjects. Theodore Roosevelt, as President, became interested and he wanted a high estandard for everything. "Even the coinage of this country came under his inspection." One evening Augustus St. Gaudens, the sculptor, was showing, at a dinner, some old golden Greek coins. Roosevelt, a guest at the dinner was immediately enthusiastic, and he then and there decided that the United States Mint should stamp a modern version of these beautiful coins. And Cortissoz asserts, "The cent, the eagle, and the double eagle, originated at that dinner with President Roosevelt."

Augustus Saint-Gaudens was an Irishman from Dublin, born in 1848, and he died in 1907. Everyone knows his statue of General Sherman at the entrance to Central Park, Sherman on horseback, and lady Victory, walking ahead, leading the way. A disgruntled Southener, seeing this statue, said, "Just like a Yankee, letting the woman do the walking, and he the riding."

Cortissoz goes on to say that the finely designed coinage led to the later reforms in coinage, such as Weiman silver pieces; Fraser's Buffalo five-cent piece; and Brenner's Lincoln penny. James Earle Fraser was an American sculptor. He made monuments and Indian statues, and designed the Indian head and buffalo for the five-cent piece in our money. Cortissoz writing about Roosevelt, "He saw that the element of art in this country was an element which bore directly upon our welfare—it added to the beauty of living, and therefore to the joy of life."

Yes, Darley liked choice company and he moved easily among such. From his picture, as the frontispiece in this book, we see him an urbane gentleman. Take a look at the New England writers around his day, and you will agree they appear countrified in comparison with this artist, Darley. Without being too worldly-wise, he seems experienced. Perhaps, an artist using his eyes, works largely outside of himself, while the writer, working inwardly with his thoughts, is more retired or retreated from the finishing touches of the world.

Lafolette's book believes that all the big fairs from the Centennial on down have been of huge advantage as points of contact between the public and both artists and artisans. Saint Gaudens' statue of Farragut, in Madison Square, New York City, had collaboration on the base from Stanford White. Admiral David Glasgow Farragut (1801-1870), was the North American Admiral of the Civil War. He was made an Admiral in 1866.

Stanford White, the American architect, lived from 1853 to 1906. He was killed by Harry Thaw in the Madison Square Garden, then at 26th Street & Madison Avenue. Stanford White did the Washington Arch, the Century and Metropolitan Clubs, New York University buildings, and the University of Virginia buildings, and many ornate private homes. He formed an association with Charles McKim and William Mead in 1881. Cortissoz in his book, tells us that Stanford White as a young man longed to be a painter, but was urged to keep to architecture as he had shown already a flair for this branch of art. White, like Darley, turned his hand to many different artistic efforts. White designed picture frames and book covers and stained glass and there is a clock designed by him, and articles of jewelry. He loved the picturesque, says Cortissoz, and went in raptures over the wax bust at Lille, and again he was overwhelmed by the "descriptive magnificence of the Book of Job."

Darley was born in the successful term of James Monroe, and his career ended during the equally successful and progressive period of Grover Cleveland. The sensitive artist that Darley was, he must have felt acutely the growing pains of the nation in all matters, but especially in art. He went steadily on, exhibiting each year at the Academy of Design and everywhere meeting with praise for his fine careful work.

In the Advertising Directory for 1833, "New York As It Is," there is a list of artists given—Thomas Cole, Landscape and Historical Painter, 1 Wall Street; A. B. Durand, Engraver, 80 Anthony Street; W. R. Hamilton, Portrait Painter, Broadway, cor, Anthony Street; William Main, Engraver, 35 Murray Street; Samuel F. B. Morse, Historical & Portrait Painter, 2 Pine Street; Rawdon Wright, Hatch & Co., Engravers, 35 Merchants Exchange; N. Rogers, Miniature Painter, 1 Cortland Street; Town, Dakin & Davis, Architects, Clinton Hall, corner of Beekman & Nassau Streets.

There is also advertised here, Artists' Colourman, with two under this heading: Disturnell, John, dealer in fine engravings, lithographs, etc., 155 Broadway; Gayward, William, importer and publisher of English engravings. The trade supplied at wholesale, 128 Broadway, upstairs.

In Doggett's New York City Directory—1849-1850, New York—Caleb Woodhull was then Mayor of New York. The American Art Union was given as 497 Broadway. The National Academy of Design was located then at 348 Broadway, announcing exhibits annually a large collection of paintings by living artists. The Council was given as A. B. Durand, President; C. C. Ingham, Vice-Presidency; J. H. Shegogue, Cor. Sec.; F. R. Spencer, Rec. Sec.; T. S. Cummings Treasurer.

In Wilson's Business Directory of New York City, 1872,

under Artists and Decorators, is the well-known name of Joel Barlow, at 103 William Street. Also advertised here is a long list of dealers in Artists' Materials, twenty or more. Among these are: Goupil & Co., 170 Fifth Avenue; M. Knoedler & Co., Successors. Then come the names of ten under the heading, Artists Scenic and Panoramic. Then a long list appears of Painters in many lines such as, Carriage, House, & Sign (numbers of the latter) Ship Painters. Then is given a list of the high-toned ones—Genre. Here is Edwin Blashfield, 6 Astor Place. Then comes Heraldic Painters. Then, next, the Historical, listing Winslow Homer, 30 University Building. Then, the Landscape Limners, in great number, among them Albert Bierstadt, 51 W. 10th St; John F. Kensett, 59 E. 23rd St., Louis Tiffany, 52 E. 23rd St. Then comes a list of Miniature Painters, among them—Charlotte Daley, 763 Broadway. Then is a List under the title, Ornamental. Then, Portrait Painters in goodly number. Among such: Thomas Hicks, 6 Astor Place; P. R. Ryder, 212 Fifth Avenue. Under Photographs, is Mathew Brady, 785 Broadway, but in the 1850 Directory, Brady had a full page ad about his Gallery of Daguerreotypes, 205 & 207 Broadway, corner of Broadway and Fulton St., and in this early ad, he announces that he "has just returned from Washington with his interesting collection of daguerreotypes of the most distinguished men of the day, including the Cabinets of Presidents Taylor and Polk, and in groups the Members of the Senate and the House, and other distinguished citizens, and these are now being exhibited at his showrooms where he should be pleased if the public would call, and examine them." And further is the announcement that Mr. Brady had just been awarded the first premium for plain and colored daguerreotypes, the third time in three successive years.

And in 1872, in the Wilson Directory, Brady had graduated to photographers with Napoleon Sarony's name among them, at 689 Broadway. Photographic Instruments and Apparatus are also advertised here, also Photographic Chemicals, and Photo Albums, and E. &. H. T. Anthony & Co., seemed to be able to supply almost anything in the photographic line, at 591 Broadway. As noted before, Brady took photographs of Darley.

To go away back, we Americans had a World's Fair, our first, in 1853-54, and in a Crystal Palace of our own, no less, right in New York City where Bryant Park and the splendid Public Library now stand, at Fifth Avenue and 42nd Street. It was the first World's Fair held in this country. To be sure, it was copied after the great Exposition in the Crystal Palace at London, in 1851. That Crystal Palace Fair was a symbol of peace, we are told, but our 1853-54 Fair was to show the progress this country had made. President Pierce was in office then, and he came up from Washington and opened the Fair, July 14, 1853, a very hot showery day. Art and industry both were displayed at this Fair. Hiram Powers' "Greek Slave," was the great attraction. Thorwaldsen, the Danish artist, had a special section for his statues and bas-reliefs, and "Christ and the Twelve Apostles," was a special attraction. It has been said that there were a number of paintings exhibited here, but mostly from artists abroad. The important artists here did not like the idea of having their works exhibited along with commercial wares, and so did not exhibit, but most people were pleased with the whole fair.

Hiram Powers (1805-1873) was the very popular American sculptor. He was abroad much of his time. His famous "Greek Slave," created much enthusiasm all over the world.

Albert Bertel Thorvaldsen or Thorwalsen (1770-1844) was the Danish sculptor who carved "The Lion of Lucerne."

This World's Fair of 1853-54 was not as financially successful as it had hoped it would be. It was a "first," in our history, something to be proud of. When the fair closed, the building was then leased to various organizations, such as, the Book Publishers Association, and then for the celebration of the Atlantic Cable of Cyrus Field, etc. On October 8th, 1858, a fire broke out in this building then full of people, in the afternoon. Everyone was gotten out safely, but the building burned to the ground in half an hour.

When the 1964 World's Fair opened in New York, the New York Times put out an interesting section, called, "A Century of Great Fairs in America as Reported in the pages of the New York Times." The Crystal Palace Fair opens this saga, reported verbatim from the New York Daily Times, July 15th, 1853. And the newspaper then cost two cents! Both the London and the New York Crystal Palaces are reviewed in a special column.

The New York Times then gives a three page verbatim account of the Centennial Exposition, in Philadelphia, 1876, A century of Independence. (with illustrations) Wednesday, May 10, 1876, was Opening Day. President Grant and Mrs. Grant came up for the event. Dom Pedro and his Empress also were present. Theodore Thomas' Band furnished the music, with a Centennial Inauguration March, by Richard Wagner, As the Times reporter there stated, it was the people who were the great attraction—people from everywhere in this country, and further away than that. John Greenleaf Whittier composed the Centennial Hymn, for the opening day. The well-known words of this Centennial Hymn have come down to us:

> "Our fathers' God! from out whose hand
> The centuries fall like grains of sand,
> We meet today, united, free,
> And loyal to our land and Thee,
> To thank Thee for the era done,
> And trust Thee for the opening one."

John Greenleaf Whittier (1807-1892) was the well-known New England poet. It was appropriate for this Quaker poet to write the hymn to be sung in the City of Brotherly Love, founded by another Quaker, William Penn.

The painting, "The Spirit of '76," with its famous drummer boy, was a feature of the fair. It now hangs in Marblehead, Massachusetts. Darley's picture exhibited at this Centennial Fair was, "A Street Scene in Rome," and was very well received by the critics and the public. Everyone agrees that the weather during the whole time of the Centennial Fair was frightful. From May to November, the thermometer registered from ninety to one hundred and over in degrees.

The Crystal Palace in London, used as a Museum, was torn down in 1941, because it aided enemy bombers. The Times in its Great Fairs section, goes on to other fairs after the Centennial in 1876. Of course, the Columbian Exposition in 1893. And someone figured out that you could go to that great Fair, by railroad, stay at some place, eat three meals, see all or most of the features at the Fair for about $76! This was for six days! Well, that was in 1893!

Then came the Pan-American Exposition, in Buffalo, where the President, William McKinley, was shot. This tragedy brought Theodore Roosevelt into the White House.

Then there was the Universal Exposition at St. Louis, 1904, with its song that has lasted down to to-day, "Meet Me in St. Louis, Louis." This Exposition was in honor of the Louisiana Purchase. Sousa's Band played here.

Next was the Panama-Pacific Exposition, in San Francisco, 1915. President Wilson, in Washington, opened this fair by wireless. That was a new trick.

Then Chicago had its turn again, with The Century of Progress, in 1933. Postmaster-General Farley opened this fair, with airplanes up overhead, roaring a welcome.

The Golden Gate Exposition, 1939, opened at San Francisco with the Pageant of the Pacific.

Then, The World of Tomorrow, New York's World Fair of 1939, with President Franklin Roosevelt dedicating it. The Trylon and the Perisphere were the symbols of this Fair.

1962, the Seattle Fair, with President Kennedy opening it with a signal beam from a star, ushering in the Space Age.

Then, the greatest Fair of all—the New York World's Fair, 1964, to honor the three hundredth birthday of New York. On September, 1664, the British took New Amsterdam away from the Dutch, and then renamed it, New York, in honor of the Duke of York, to whom his brother, Charles II had given it. This Fair is an amazing sight, an adventure into many lands and among various peoples. It has everything. The exhibits sent on from other lands are great attractions, especially the Pieta at the Vatican Pavilion, particularly as Italy is celebrating the Four Hundredth Anniversary this year of the sculptor and genius who did this marvelous work, the Pieta—Michelangelo. Michelangelo (Buonarroti) (1475-1564), the Italian artist, and one of the greatest figures of the Italian Renaissance, and of the world in art.

Much can be expected to result from this Exposition of 1964 in New York, out at the Flushing Meadows. We are on the high road now, with foreign visitors eager to give out what they know, and eager to learn what they can at this mighty center. It is more than a mart, it is a realization of past hopes and a dream of the future.

CHAPTER V

Travels Abroad

ALTHOUGH DARLEY did much important traveling about in the cities of the Eastern States of this country, in connection with his art work, his reflective eye gently observing all that was to be seen, he did not go abroad until he was mature—so busy was he with orders here, and with small time for vacations. It was not until the 1860's that he took time out to go to Europe, and he was then in his alert but ripened forties. He was known by reputation for a long while in the art circles and to the general public of most of the European cities. Many important ones in the book mart there were eager to make connections with him. So probably it was some of these receptive ones who got him to visit abroad, for a vacation as well as for orders and prospects.

With his wife, he took the steamer, "Cuba" and set forth to explore another world about which he had already formed good opinions. During this enjoyable trip which he felt he must share with dear ones left behind in his home land, he started, even aboard ship, to write little descriptive letters, picking out the high points of his itinerary, and in sometimes droll, but always effective wording, put down his impressions—in a way, make miniature sketches and brief word-pictures for his separated relatives and friends to give them the chance to go along with him in imagination. These letters were so much enjoyed by those who received them, that he was urged to publish them. He was reluctant to do this, considering the brief notes simply private correspondence without much appeal to the public at large. But his friends wanted these illustrated missives made permanent part of current events through publication, and at last he gave in to this urgent encouragement, and apologizing for the letters' informality, he did have them published in a small book, called,—"Sketches Abroad With Pen and Pencil," by Felix O. C. Darley. The book is most interesting with accompanying drawings. And in the way he has handled the telling prose, makes the sketch book a delightfully readable book on travel and art. The book was published by Hurd and Houghton, Cambridge, Riverside Press, in 1868. The drawings in the book were engraved on wood by J. Agustus Bogart and James L. Langridge. As a preface to the book, Darley has this—A Word to the Reader, that the book was not meant for "the public eye," but for "the eye domestic," simply "extracts from familiar letters from abroad, to friends and relatives at home." He apologizes by saying, "I have sketched only and finished nothing, and trust that amiable body known as the Public will look upon my shortcomings in this extremely mild literary effort with an indulgent eye," Sept. 1868.

And thus the book starts, aboard ship steamboat "Cuba," June 18, 186-. He is up on deck taking a polite but keen look around. It does not seem long before he picks out characters and sketches them into the reader's memory with a few incisive strokes. There is the elderly gentleman stretched out on a deck chair, covered with a plaid shawl, his felt hat tied under his chin, under which hat nothing can be seen but a nose. But the sagging picture the old fellow makes is one of patient suffering.

Another one comes up on deck, but this one on his feet, a tall angular clergyman from the West, and immediately Darley notes his, "small, penetrating blue eyes whose glance enters your brain like a gimlet."

Then Darley's own sharp eyes discover a whale rolling along near the ship, "shining like an immense dark bottle."

Another group that attracts Darley's attention is composed of some British soldiers, smoking and playing cards in a nonchalant way, oblivious to surroundings. And Darley notes and sketches the "knowing" little caps on their heads. The word, "knowing," is such a good word here, the reader catches the relief of soldiers at ease.

After the landing, Darley begins his description of the tour—starting with brief account of Chester, the oldest town in England, settled by the Romans. He cites the Cathedral there, built away back in the 10th Century, and he tells of the tower on the wall around the city and that on this tower Charles I watched the defeat of his army by Cromwell, at the Battle of Marston Moor. And Darley goes on to mention an old house in this region, when he was there, that escaped the Great Plague, and bearing this inscription, "God's Providence Is Mine Inheritance."

Then Darley's party visited Eton Hall, the seat of the Marquis of Westminster, considered the most imposing place in England. In the dining room hang pictures by Raphael, and family portraits by Reynolds, West, Gainsborough. This must have been an adventure for Darley.

The next entry in this travel book is Tintern Abbey, "a poem in stone." This is the old Abbey that Wordsworth wrote his poem about. Everyone knows these lines:

"Nature never did betray the heart that loved her; 'tis
  her privilege
Through all the years of this our life, to lead
From joy to joy; for she can so inform
The mind that is within us, so impress
With quietness and beauty, and so feed
With lofty thoughts, that neither evil tongues,
Rash judgments, nor the sneers of selfish men,
Nor greetings where no kindness is, nor all
The dreary intercourse of daily life,
Shall e'er prevail against us, nor disturb
Our cheerful faith."

60

LAST WORDS OF CAPTAIN NATHAN HALE, THE HERO AND MARTYR
OF THE AMERICAN REVOLUTION

Then, Darley is at Exeter, June 22, where the cathedral was with the oak throne of the Bishops.

And then, London, June 29th Darley visits Westminster Abbey, and The Poets Corner—among them, Gray, Pope, Addison, Chaucer, Browning, Tennyson, and scores more. In this Abbey, all the Kings and Queens of England have been crowned since William the Conqueror. Two shields hang there, used at the battles of Agincourt and Crecy. At Agincourt, Henry V defeated the French, August 25th, 1415. And at the Battle of Crecy, the English defeated the French in 1346. Darley is enthralled with Hyde Park's dashing equipages, and the equestrians on horseback to keep order in the admiring crowds.

Another day, Darley reports, he was at Hampton Court Palace, enjoying the hundreds of pictures there. This Palace was built by Cardinal Wolsey, 1515. In the great Hall that was used as a theatre in the reigns of Charles I and James I, some of Shakespeare's plays were first acted. The walls were hung with arras tapestry representing scenes from the Life of Abraham. Among the portraits were those of Henry VIII, Cardinal Wolsey, Queen Elizabeth, and Jane Seymour, all Lely's portraits of the beauties of the Court of Charles II, and a number of Van Dykes and Kellners. Darley thought Lely's portraits were stiff and affected. Sir Peter Lely (1618-85), was the Dutch portrait painter. His real name was Pieter van der Faes. He came after Van Dyke as the English Court painter. But Darley considered Holbein's Henry VIII "full of that intense individuality which characterized all his works."

Still in London, Darley attended services at the Middle Temple Church in Temple Bar. Lord Brougham was there that day, and looked "aged and infirm." Lord Brougham (1778-1868), was the English Statesman and scholar. In 1802, he with others founded the Edinburgh Review. Darley notes that in the graveyard at this Middle Temple Church was the tomb of Oliver Goldsmith, with the simple inscription, "Here lies Oliver Goldsmith."

Then Darley visited the famous Dulwich Gallery with its many pictures. He found among these, "some admirable Guidos, Murillos, Van Dykes, etc."

The Royal Academy of Arts was founded by the King himself, George III, in 1769. It is said that Benjamin West urged him on to this. Sir Joshua Reynolds was the first president there, but our own Benjamin West enjoyed that honor likewise, of being president of the Academy.

Darley was surprised at some of the fine works of Landseer that he saw at the Royal Academy. Darley thought these very charming, "showing wonderful freedom and truth, much better than I expected, as I had always understood Landseer's pictures were poor in color." Sir Edwin Henry Landseer (1802-73), was the English animal painter.

It was a glorious treat for Darley to visit the National Gallery in London. He writes, "The first picture that forcibly struck me as I entered the room, was a splendid head by Rembrandt—great, would be the better expression—so full of life, it almost seemed to think." A "Portrait of a Gentleman," by Van Dyke, was to Darley, a work of genius. So did Velasquez's portrait of Philip of Spain. He also greatly admired several more heads by Rembrandt, "all fine, especially one of himself as an old man—also a fine Turner next to a Claude." But he is somewhat disappointed in Claude. This Claude Lorraine, whose real name was Claude Gelee or Gellee, was a French painter who lived from 1600-1682. He was known for his landscapes, all light and distance. He settled in Rome under the patronage of Pope Urban VIII.

Darley visited the Kensington Museum in London with its great variety of articles, and fine portraits of the English School from Reynolds to the present (186). This place also has celebrated cartoons of Raphael. Here, too, was Wilkie's exquisite "Village Festival," and "Blind Fiddler," and

Hogarth's works which showed "a wonderful power of invention and knowledge of character."

Nor did the tourist Darley miss a trip to the Tower. Visiting the Horse Armory, he saw a suit of Greek armor, two thousand years old, with a helmet like Minerva's. And he also saw, with horror, the axe used in the executions of Lady Jane Grey and Anne Boleyn.

A little later Darley explored Kenilworth Castle that Queen Elizabeth bestowed on her favorite, the Earl of Leicester. At Stratford he noted the lovely Avon River, blue then, and not sudsy with the detergents the women about use to wash clothing. He visited Shakespeare's house, and the church, and then the cottage of Anne Hathaway, Shakespeare's senior by seven or eight years. But then Shakespeare was someone apart, probably a mature man at his marriage at eighteen years, and caring not at all for girls in their teens. Darley would have a personal interest in Shakespeare, for, along with Alonzo Chappell, he illustrated the Bard's Dramas. Oh, there was so much for Darley to see all about, and for his artful pencil to sketch.

There was Guy's cliff, with its legend that Guy de Beauchamp, Earl of Warwick, in remose for having killed such a number of men in battle, had hewed himself a cave out of the solid rock, and lived alone there for thirty years, doing penance for his sins. Oh, this mighty Guy!' He appealed to Darley. Perhaps he would have liked to sketch him, such a man, nine feet tall, the tale goes, with a breast-plate three feet long and weighing thirty-five pounds. The shield could hardly be raised by an average man's two hands. But it was easy enough for Guy who weilded a sword of twenty pounds. We see Darley intensely interested in details as he runs over these mighty items, ending up with the stupendous size of Guy's porridge pot that held one hundred and twenty gallons and weighed eight hundred and three pounds.

Then, after the date, August 6th—Haddon Hall, a very

interesting place, this seat of the Vernons. From here Dorothy Vernon eloped with her lover, Sir John Manners. And Darley remarks that the chapel here has stained glass windows with the date on them, 1424, long before Christopher Columbus discovered America.

By August 12th, Darley was at Canterbury. Hardwick Hall, was built in Elizabeth's reign by the famous "Bess of Hardwick." Darley attended services at St. Martin's, the oldest church in England, where Saint Paul is said to have preached. So much that is picturesque there, Darley notes. The very large Cathedral is beautiful, and the spot where Thomas a Becket was murdered is pointed out. Thomas a Becket (1118-70), was Archbishop of England, but dissensions arose, and he was murdered in the Cathedral. Darley writes, "Every foot of England seems to have history."

And then comes Paris, August 15th—Napoleon's birthday. The Champs Elysees from the Place de la Concorde to Arc de Triomphe, the famous Avenue of Paris, "all was life and movement everywhere." Darley's eyes caught it all, and perhaps his ready pencil caught some of this life, in swift drawings. The Arc de Triomphe commemorates Napoleon's victories. Built in 1806 to 1816, from plans by J. F. Chalgrin.

Darley was traveling swiftly and eagerly. By August 19th he was at Geneva—visiting the beautiful Lake Leman or Lake Geneva that has so often been sung of and written about, with charming scenery and vineyard shores. Mont Blanc, the highest of the Alps was originally called the Montaine Mauduit. In 1694 the name, Mont Blanc, as applied to it, was found in an Italian document. Darley proceeds to Chillon the Castle there built, 9th to 13th century, now is a museum. Everyone is familiar with Byron's Sonnet, on Chillon, beginning—

> "Eternal Spirit of the chainless mind,
> Brightest in dungeons, Liberty! thou art
> For there thy habitation is the heaet."

Byron lived from 1788 to 1824. Francois de Bonnivarde—1493-1570, was the hero of Byron's Sonnet, "The Prisoner of Chillon." Darley sees Byron's name cut in the stone rock there by Byron himself.

The next stop for Darley was Vevey, Switzerland, August 29th. Here he sketches the Shrines along the wayside, with passersby kneeling down to pray at them.

By September 9th, he is in the Rhone Valley, watching the women at work in the fields. Then, by October 1st, the Valley of the Rhine—Munich with its vast Cathedral. Munich, the capital of Bavaria, was built up by its Kings as an art center. "The Glyptothek, a splendid building, was erected by King Ludwig in 1816, an art gallery to contain both ancient and modern sculpture—The Sleeping Faun—Bacchus, etc. The old Pinacothek held the works of the Old Masters." One large room hung with Rubens works, alone, and his portraits "a great master of color and composition." His "Falling Angels," is a marvelous work, and "his portraits are painted with great force and freedom." Peter Paul Rubens (1577-1640), master of all Flemish School of painting. His "Venus and Adonis" is at the Metropolitan Museum in New York City. Here also are many Rembrandts that Darley takes delight in. Another point about Munich is the way the dogs are made to work there and put to much use. He liked dogs.

By October 6, he was in Nuremburg, in Northern Bavaria, the birthplace of Albrecht Durer, and Darley writes of the bronze statue erected to him, "Evangelist of Art." Durer lived from 1471 to 1508. Longfellow wrote the poem, "Nuremburg"—

From Longfellow's Poem, *Nuremburg*

Here, when Art was still religious,
  with a simple, reverent heart,
Lived and labored Albrecht Durer,
  the Evangelist of Art;

Not thy Councils, not thy Kaisers, win
for thee the world's regard;
But thy painter, Albrecht Durer, and
Hans Sachs, thy cobbler bard.

Hans Sachs—(1494-1576)—the shoemaker and German meistersinger, and he wrote plays and poems, and is the principal character in Wagner's opera, Die Meistersinger.

Darley illustrated Longfellow's works. In this present book are three of these illustrations, two from "Evangeline," and one from "The Village Blacksmith."

By the 21st of October, Darley was at Baden-Baden, and he tells here that at Frankfort he had seen the house from the window of which Luther addressed the people prior to his journey to Worms. And Darley mentions the statue of Schiller at Munich. Friedrich von Schiller (1759-1805) was the German poet. He was a friend of Goethe. Schiller's best known and favorite ballad is, "The Song of the Bell."

At Heidelberg, Darley recalls, was the Great Heidelberg Tun which held sixty thousand gallons, of wine. Heidelberg is on the Necker River with its beautiful scenery. The University of Heidelberg was founded in 1386, but Darley found nothing "remarkable about the large building." He notes that "the students wore small caps of different colors, to designate the different clubs to which they belonged." Baden-Baden, the famous spa, had the well-known gambling house, Kursaal Rouge et Noir. This city is said to have been founded by Hadrian, in the Second Century, A.D. He was the Roman Emperor, and lived from 76-138 A.D.

By now Darley had found out that Sunday is the liveliest day in Europe. He writes from Amsterdam, October 29th, that after he left Baden-Baden, he went on to Strasbourg and saw the famous Cathedral there, with its remarkable clock. This Catholic Cathedral was built from 1015 to 1439. From Strasbourg, Darley and his party proceeded to Mayence on the Rhine, the beautiful river often compared to New

York's Hudson River. He saw, too, the Mouse Tower of Bishop Hatto, about whom is told the story that he was devoured by rats because he had compared the cry of the poor to the squeaking of mice. Darley also visited the Castle of Ehrenfeld on the left, and the Castle of the Two Brothers beyond. Darley was missing nothing now that he had started on the long-delayed trip. Going along, dreaming, sketching or planning sketches, probably taking orders along the way, it must have been a most enjoyable as well as a rewarding journey. To see things at last he had often heard of in rapturous tones—like, the Rhine by moonlight, that was a prize worth coming to win.

Then on to Cologne, whence comes the reviving Eau de Cologne. And there was the Cathedral, famed through the years, a prize winner in Gothic architecture. Work on this Cathedral began in the 13th Century. The Reformation caused hard times. But in 1823, renovation on it began and it was opened in 1880. In this Cathedral is the Shrine of the Three Kings of Cologne, thought to be the Wise Kings whose bones were brought there by Frederick Barbarossa. Frederick I, known as Barbarossa (1123-1190). Barbarossa means, "Red Beard." On another day, Darley saw the Church of St. Ursula in Cologne, that holds the bones of the eleven thousand Virgins who accompanied St. Ursula on her trip to Rome and the Holy Places. There is the legend in the Vatican that Ursula was the daughter of a Christian King of Great Britain. When she and her companions reached Cologne, they were killed by the Huns. She is considered the Patroness of young maidens.

Then next in the itinerary of Darley came Dusseldorf, the place where Henrich Heine was born, (1797-1856). He was a German of Jewish parents. He was a great poet. No one can forget his "Lorelei." Many of the foremost musicians—Schubert, Schumann, Mendelssohn, etc. have written music for his lyrics.

After Dusseldorf, the next step for Darley was Amsterdam, in North Holland. This was where Rembrandt lived. Darley testified that, "the art galleries are admirable," and he sets down in particular of seeing Rembrandt's "Night Watch." Harmenszoom van Ryn Rembrandt, (1606-1669). He was born at Leyden, but in 1631 went to live in Amsterdam. His picture, "Sortie of the Banning-Cocq Company," was called, in mockery, "The Night Watch," because of its artistic unconventionality in focusing the bright light on a few central figures, and leaving the rest in shadow.

By now, the swift-footed Darley was in Antwerp, and he writes, "From Amsterdam, I went on to the Hague." And, "In South Holland, many outstanding Rembrandts there," and he remarks especially, Rembrandt's, "Professor Tulp lecturing over a dead body to his pupils," and Darley is in raptures over this, "a wonderful work for color and truth. The head of the Professor is inimitable." Darley notes, too, that Paul Potter's "Bull," is there, too, but he seemed to think, "it had a dry and bald look," Paul (Paulus) Potter, (1623-54), was the Dutch artist who did animal pictures with much simplicity and artlessness.

At Antwerp, Belgium, Darley went to St. Jacques' Church to see Rubens' tomb there, and the picture that this artist painted, and which hangs above it, one of his first pictures. Antwerp was Rubens home, and here, too, Van Dyke was born. Peter Paul Rubens (1577-1640). Darley goes on to describe the Church of St. Jacques as, "elaborately ornamental, filled with statues and pictures, many by Van Dyke." Anthony Van Dyke, (1590-1641), was born at Antwerp, and his teacher was Rubens. His "Crucifixion," is in the Cathedral at Mechlin. In the Antwerp Cathedral, Darley saw the greatest of Rubens Works, "The Descent from the Cross," and, "The Elevation of the Cross," Darley liked the latter more than, "The Descent from the Cross." In the "Elevation of the Cross," he thought the head of Christ was noble in expression. Darley noted the Museum's collection of Old Masters. And he goes on to tell of an artist he saw there in the Museum copying one of Rubens pictures, with his foot. Born without arms, he made an admirable copy, and Darley further states that this capable man could write well, too.

A short time later, the tireless Darley is back in Paris again, and he tells that after leaving Antwerp, he saw Ghent, Bruges, and Brussels. Ghent is in Flanders, North Belgium. The Treaty of Ghent, signed, December 24, 1814, ended our War of 1812. Darley attended Vespers at the Church of the Beguniage, a group of small Convents with about seven hundred nuns doing charitable work. Bruges, Darley declares, is very interesting, the oldest of Flemish towns. It is in Northwest Belgium. It once was an international port. The Hospital of St. John, 12th Century, has works of Hans Memling, (1430-1494), a religious painter. Darley feels the charm in these old cities, recalling to mind Froissart's Chronicles, Jean Froissart, (1337-1410?) These literary tales bring the past to life.

Brussels, Darley feels, is more like Paris, "light and glittering." When one thinks of Brussels, the word, "lace," comes to mind—Brussels lace—also Brussels sprouts. Brussels was Wellington's headquarters in the Waterloo Campaign. Recall Byron's—

> "There was a sound of revelry by night,
> And Belgium's capital had gathered then
> Her beauty and her chivalry, and bright
> The lamps shone o'er fair women and brave men.
> A thousand hearts beat happily; and when
> Music arose with its voluptuous swell,
> Soft eyes looked love to eyes which spoke again.
> And all went merry as a marriage bell.
> But hush! Hark! a deep sound strikes like
> a rising knell!"

> From: *The Eve of the Battle of Waterloo.*
> (*Child Harold's Pilgrimage*)

69

Then Darley writes again from Paris, November 18th. He went to the Louvre and enjoyed the pictures there very much. This French Museum was put up in 1204, as a fortress palace, and finally converted into a museum by Napoleon. Leonardo's, "Mona Lisa," is there. Leonardo da Vinci, (1479-1576), was born in Vinci, Italy. Darley saw also at the Louvre, Titian's, "Man With the Glove," Titian, (1479-1576), was the genius of Venice in art, a sumptuous style was high of the High Renaissance. Darley tells of the Rubens there at the Louvre, and the Van Dykes—Van Dyke's Charles I "looked every inch a king." The theatre, too, attracted Darley, while in Paris, and he called it extremely French, the draperies short and light. And, then, of course, the Luxembourg had to be visited, and here he rejoices in the fact that this picture gallery has some of the best modern art.

Then, December 17th, to the Ecole des Beaux Arts, founded in 1642, with free instruction for those qualified by passing an entrance examination. Painting and graphic arts, sculpture and architecture are taught there, all the fine arts. A competition is held here each year for the students to compete for the Grand Prix de Rome. Did Darley sigh that he had missed the training given in this celebrated school of art? We wonder. Here at the Ecole des Beaux Arts, Darley saw and admired Delaroche's "The Hemiscycle," Paul (Hyppolyte) Delaroche (1797-1856), was the French historic painter.

Darley tells that Dore, the artist, was at the American Minister's Reception. Gustave Dore (1833-1883) was the French artist who painted very large canvases, like, "Christ Entering into Jerusalem." He also illustrated many books—Don Quixote, Dante, LaFontaine, Tennyson, Milton, the Bible. Darley writes that he also met at this Reception, Bulwer, and he must have meant, Bulwer-Lytton, and, as Darley puts it, "suggesting Mephistopheles." Bulwer-Lytton

(1803-1873), wrote "The "Last Days of Pompeii," 1834, "Eugene Aram," 1833, and the play, "The Lady of Lyons." His son wrote under the pen name of "Owen Meredith."

Then Darley is again at the Louvre, admiring the pictures. "Some of the best Guidos," he saw there, and he writes, "Veronese's, "Marriage of Cana," a miracle of Venetian art, thirty feet long." Paolo Veronese (1528-1588), was born at Verona. Furthermore Darley goes in raptures over the antique sculptures in the Louvre, especially over the beautiful "Venus de Milo," and he calls this, "the greatest ideal of woman ever discovered—majestic but not lovable."

By December 25th, he is at Genoa, calling this city venerable and dirty. On the way to Genoa, he had stopped at Marseilles, and also at Nice, the latter, "a pleasant cheerful town with a soft climate." In the village near Genoa, he was shown the house where Christopher Columbus was born. Darley and his party, went to Midnight Mass, Christmas Eve, in the Cathedral of San Lorenzo. Genoa is on the Mediterranean Sea. Besides Columbus, Paganini, the famous violinist, also was born at Genoa. He was also a composer, and is remembered for his piece, "Perpetual Motion." Niccolo Paganini, (1782-1842). Darley refers to the Knights of Malta. They were probably honorary attendants at the Midnight Mass. This is a religious society of laymen. In the olden days of the Crusades, they were the Knights-Hospitalers.

By December 30th, Darley was at Pisa. In the lovely Tuscan city, Galileo was born. Of course, Darley did not miss seeing the Leaning Tower of Pisa, built of marble, commenced in 1174, and finished in 1350. It leans thirteen feet out of the perpendicular. And, to be sure, he saw the Duomo and the old Cathedral and the Baptistry. Pisa is on the River Arno that flows into the Tyrolean Sea. Darley also writes of the Campo Santo, the burial ground filled with earth brought from the Holy Land. And in this resting place, are many "noble families interred."

71

Then, at last, it is Darley's turn to enter the Eternal City. Rome, January 6, 1867. Before arriving there he had been at Florence, and what a city that was. Scores of famous ones were born or had lived and worked there—Dante, Boccaccio, Fra Angelico, Da Vinci, Michelangelo, Raphael, etc., etc. But once in Rome, all else was forgotten by Darley. Although he was somewhat disappointed with St. Peter's. Then there was the Palace of the Caesars, a mass of ruins—then the Coliseum, the largest Roman amphitheatre. It could hold fifty thousand. Built between 72 A.D. and 82 A.D., here the gladiators held their combats. Then there was the Arch of Constantine. Yes, Rome was eternal, with everything to be seen.

January 13, Darley went to the Church of Ara Coeli where the Holy Bambino was. He also beheld the terrifying Tarpeian Rock from which criminals were thrown, and bears the dreadful name of Tarpeia, the Roman woman who betrayed her city to the Sabines for the gift of gold bracelets. Another sight for Darley was the Basilica of St. John Lateran where all the Popes are crowned. This is the Cathedral of Rome, the Pope's Church. Darley went three times to the Vatican. The Vatican is a collection of buildings in Rome grouped around the residence of the Pope on Vatican Hill. Then there is the Sistine Chapel, built in 1473, with Michelangelo's frescoes on the ceiling; his Last Judgment on a wall. Darley visited the Capitol once. In the Vatican he saw the Apollo Belvedere, the Laocoon, and the Torso. The Sistine Chapel seemed his favorite delight, especially noted Fra Angelico's "Last Judgment," the "Creation of Adam," and Darley remarks further, "Jonah is very good." The Picture Gallery, he goes on, has "The Transfiguration," of Raphael. Raffaello Sanzio (1483-1520). His father was Court Painter to the Duke of Urbino. Raphael was born in this Urbino. When he worked in Rome, he had Pope Leo X as his patron. Perhaps his best known work is the "Sistine

Madonna." Here, too, in the Picture Gallery, Darley saw Domenichino's "Saint Jerome." This painter, 1581-1641, was an Italian painter of the Carracci School. At the Capitol, Darley noted "The Dying Gladiator," and, "The Fawn," by Praxitiles, and he adds, "Exquisite." Praxitiles was the renowned Greek Sculptor (370 to 330 B.C.)

CHAPTER VI

Steel Engravings

DARLEY WAS IN ROME, January 18. He writes, "Yesterday we went to see the donkeys and horses blessed by the Pope, in front of the Church of San Antonio." And again to the Capitol to see the Picture Gallery—"a fine head of Velasquez, by himself." Diego Rodrigo Velasquez (1599-1660). When he went to Madrid he was Court Painter to Philip IV. He visited Italy, and the first time there he painted, "The Forge of Vulcan," and on the second trip, the Portrait of "Pope Innocent X." Also at this picture Gallery, Darley saw and noted a large altar-piece by Guercino, "a work of great power." This Guercino whose real name was Giovanni Barbiere, born 1591, and died 1666. It is said that he shows in his work the influence of Guido.

In the Barberini Palace Darley saw the "Beatrice Cenci," which has bewitched the world for two centuries. "She seemed only a pretty woman," remarks Darley, "slightly sad." Then they went on to St. Peter's to witness the Festival of St. Peter's Chair. The Catholic Dictionary explains the Chair of St. Peter, thus: "This portable chair preserved at the Vatican, and believed to be a chair used by St. Peter, the extant testimony referring to it dating to the 2nd Century. The Feast of the Chair of St. Peter at Rome has been celebrated from the early days of the Christian Era on January 18th, in commemoration of the day when St. Peter held his first service in Rome. The Feast of the Chair of St. Peter at Antioch commemorating his founding the See at Antioch,

74

has also been long celebrated at Rome, Feb. 22. The Mass for both days is the same."

Darley is next heard from in Naples, January 26th. The great Vesuvius! On August 24th, A.D. 79, it erupted, destroying the towns of Pompeii and Herculaneum. That was the first on record, and Pliny, the Younger, the Roman statesman, described this eruption in a letter to Tacitus, the Roman historian (55-117 A.D.). Pliny the Younger lived from about 60 A.D. to about 113 A.D. Vesuvius was quiet enough when Darley was there, evidently.

January 31st, he and his party greet Sorrento on its rocky base. It was here in the lush grape-land, that the poet Tasso was born and lived (1544-95). Torquato Tasso was the Italian poet who wrote *Jerusalem Delivered*. Then came Cyprus, the beautiful island in the Bay of Naples. It was Greek once, then later, Roman. Then on to Salerno, where once a great medical school flourished, started in the 9th Century. The next point of travel for Darley was Paesteum, once a Greek City. It is on the Bay of Salerno. Excavators have uncovered ancient civilization there. And then Eboli, and then again to Rome with its fascinating attractions. There were the Baths of the old Roman Emperor (188-217). It was said he was called, Caracallo, after his Gallic tunic. His rightful name was Marcus Aurelius Cintonumus. Then the Church of St. Clement of San Cappucine, The Friars Minor. Capuchine means hooded. The members of this Order wear the robes and hoods. Then Darley proceeded to Borghese Palace, which was the winter residence of the Borghese family, and later a Picture Gallery. The Borghese were a great Roman family. They had many Cardinals among their members, and even a Pope, Pope Paul V. Darley saw many things in Rome. Statues for one—The great Pompey's (106 B.C.-45 B.C.) The Roman General, a rival of Julius Caesar. Then February 23rd, and the Carnival in Rome prior to the beginning of Lent. This sometimes starts in Rome on Epiphany, January

75

6th, Twelfth Night, and lasts until Shrove Tuesday, the day before Ash Wednesday.

The Corso—the races—the Via Flamina, a mile long. In Carnival time the promenade of the masked and gaily attired ones tossing flowers and confetti in mimic warfare. Then the Campagna di Roma, the huge reclaimed plain surrounding Rome, now offering charming landscapes. Nero, of the many crimes (37-68 A.D.), the Roman Emperor who considered himself a poet and artist. And when he was about to die, he said, "What an artist the world is losing in me!"

Writing still from Rome, March 30th, Darley gives an account of his sight-seeing jaunts—Grotto Ferrata, Lake Albano—There is so much to see and revel in, time flies away. April 1st, he is at the Catacombs, the burial places of the early Christians, outside the City. By April 16th, Darley is in Florence. The Uffizi Palace, (1560), of Cosimo de Medici, houses one of the finest art collections in the world. Then Darley goes ga-ga over Palazzo Vecchio, a great statue of David, by Michelangelo. Then the Pitti Palace with its rare works, the Campanile by Giotto. Giotto, (1266-1337), a Florentine artist. He decorated the Campanile. The Strozzi Palace—the Ponte Vecchio over the Arno. Still roving on in this marvellous city of Florence, Darley goes to see the Church of the Lorenzo that contains two of Michelangelo's masterworks, the tombs of Lorenzo de Medici and Giulio de Medici; also the wonderful "Virgin and Child." Here is the house of Michelangelo with the inscription, "Here lived the divine Michelangelo." Vittoria Colona, Marchesa di Pescara, (1492-1547), was a poet and a friend of Michelangelo. She wrote on religion and grief after her husband's death. Darley saw and visited the Church of Santa Croce with its art treasures. The Duomo is the Cathedral of Florence. Darley saw the tombs of the mighty of Florence —Michelangelo, Dante, Galileo, Alfieri, and Machiavelli.

"CAME FROM THE NEIGHBORING HAMLETS AND FARMS THE ACADIAN WOMEN"
(from *Evangeline*, by Longfellow)

Alfieri was the Italian poet (1749-1803). Nicolo Machiavelli (1469-1527). His great work was, "The Prince."

By May 6th, Darley was in Venice, "The Bride of the Sea," when the Doges lived there. In the ceremony of investing one of these Doges, a ring was tossed into the Gulf of Venice, thus wedding the land and the sea. Venice on account of its triumphs over Cyprus, Crete, and other Greek Islands, won the title of, "Queen of the Sea." Only walkers can use the narrow foot-paths in Venice, and all other traffic is by water through the hundreds of canals and their picturesque gondolas. Darley remarked the Piazzetto of St. Mark's, and St. Mark's Church, the See of the Patriarch of Venice, also the doge's Palace, now used as an art gallery and is connected with the old prison by the Bridge of Sighs. The famous bridge, the Rialto, spans the Grand Canal. The Clock Tower—Titian—Tintoretto—Paolo Veronese, the great artist of Venice. Darley saw and wondered at Titian's great art in the picture, "The Assumption," Titian, (1477-1570). His "Holy Family," is in the Louvre, and his "Magdalen," is in the Pitti Palace in Florence, and his "Saint Margaret," is in Madrid. He painted the famous portrait of Pope Paul III. He was the foremost painter of his day, and one of the greatest of all time. Tintoretto (1518-94) was an Italian painter, probably born in Venice. His picture, "Paradise," is in the Ducal Palace in Venice. This is believed to be the largest picture on canvas in existence. Paolo Veronese (1528-88), was born in Verona, but on becoming famous was called to Venice to decorate the Ducal Palace. He painted, "Venice Enthroned," and the "Apotheosis of Venice." His "Marriage of Cana," is in the Louvre.

Before going to this delightful Venice, Darley had stopped at Padua, renowned for its great University, 1222, with the first anatomy hall in Europe. The tomb of Saint Anthony is at Padua. Darley saw the splendid equestrian statue by Donatello. Donatello lived from 1386-1466, a Florentine painter, but he made the statue for Padua.

It must have been hard to leave Italy with its soft Italian tongue, the "language used in Heaven." But, next we find Darley in Paris, June 17th. In this letter, he tells that he has been to Milan, on the way thither, and visited the Cathedral with Da Vinci's, "Last Supper." Then he had gone to Dijon, the center for Burgundy wine, then in Paris to the Great Exposition. He remarks that the American collection there is very small. He had an entry here, "The March to Fredericksburg, Virginia," and this was well received, but he does not mention this fact. But he does write about the Bois de Boulogne, and he must have seen Montmartre—long a Bohemian world. The Bois de Boulonge is one of the famous boulevards of Paris. It is a park of 2,155 acres. The Longchamps race course is there, one of the best known in the world. Darley must have been enjoying the time of his life.

He goes to London, June 22nd, but does not stop long there. Then, heading homewards, he arrives at Rouen with its memories of Joan of Arc, and, of course, the fine Cathedral of Notre Dame (13th to 15th centuries) with its two different towers. Rouen is also famous for Corneille and Flaubert, both born there. Pierre Corneille (1606-84), the French dramatist, and Gustave Flaubert (1821-80), the French novelist.

And then, the entry, Dieppe . . . and then back to native America, after an honored and much enjoyed tour. It might have been a delayed wedding trip—a transplanted one.

Dieppe is a great tourist center, a good point of departure. These letters Darley had sent back to relatives and friends were so much appreciated that he was urged to publish them, and finally, reluctantly, he consented. And his book, "Sketches with Pen and Pencil," was brought out, with the drawings engraved on wood, by J. Augustus Bogert and James Langridge, in New York, 1869, published by Hurd and Houghton, Cambridge Riverside Press. Darley with his picturesque wording and his charming sketches take the reader along with him here in a journey that is delightful, interesting, profitable, and sentimental enough to suit anyone.

Now with his European trip over, Darley, stimulated by what he saw abroad, happy in the recollection of being so well received by the great and little of Europe, successful with commissions and projects, settles down again to his steady, sure, swift mode of life, always eager for new ideas and ways to better his painting and drawing.

In, "Art in America," A Critical and Historical Sketch by S. G. W. Benjamin, author of "Contemporary Art in Europe"; "What is Art," etc., New York, Harper Brothers, publishers, 1880, then at Franklin Square, says in Chapter VI, of this book, page 104, "With us (Americans) bloom and fruition suddenly burst forth after a period of apparently unpromising barrenness," and the author points out here how West and Copley appeared almost full-fledged, fitting into important positions in Europe with but, "few premonitory signs to indicate that the country (U.S) was prepared for the advent of such artists."

In 1785, the American Magazine offered apologies for the defective prints, declaring that infancy in the arts in America was an excuse. Then, almost twenty years later, comes this, "Peter Maverick does good steel engravings, in N.Y.C.", and then years later, "A. B. Durand, was executing the masterly engravings of Trumbull's Declaration of Independence, and such."

Other arts were later here, the author tells us—such as the plastic, and, also we seemed blind to the resources of black and white. Samuel Rowse was to give impetus to crayon drawing. "Then came Schools of Landscape artists, employing charcoal." Hopkinson Smith handled charcoal in a masterly manner. "F. O. C. Darley, was one of the first to show capacity in our latest branch of art" (book illustrations). The author here says that Darley's style, "soon became very mannered." Not all critics would agree with this assertion. But the author goes on to say about Darley, "But he also shows originality and imagination in seizing striking characteristics of Americans, and a refined fancy in representing both humor and pathos." And here the author applauds Darley, saying, that his illustrations to "Rip Van Winkle," and to Judd's, "Margaret," put him among the best.

Thomas Moran was also fine in this field. "In a sudden burst of black and white, America again went to the top." Did Darley ever think of going to Japan? He did a number of banknote vignettes for the Japanese Government, and fine ones, too, like all of his work. The best of the engravers gladly did banknote engraving. Darley, always busy, could travel anywhere in imagination. He might have been thinking something like that when he was at Rouen, where La Pucelle suffered death at the stake. When she was on trial, and told of the voices she heard directing her in her course of action, the stern old judge said harshly, "Those voices you heard were only in your imagination." And Joan quickly answered him, with, "Of course, but sometimes that is the way God speaks to us." It needed imagination to draw the vignettes. It was said that the American banknote engraving was famous through all the world, and consequently much banknote engraving was done for foreign countries. This work helped along the development of art in this country. This work certainly developed craftsmanship. We hear of such triumphs of dexterity as a fascimile of the Declaration of Independence, engraved in 1840, with a pictorial border in a space only three and a quarter by one and a half inches, issued by the American Bank Note Company.

F. Weitenkampf, in his book, "American Graphic Art," says on page 149, "the increasing skill of the illustrators also

counteracted on the engravers—not only was facsimile reproduction of pencil drawings called for, but washes placed on
the block by the artist, had to be represented by lines. That
developed interpretation." The "Sketch Book," of Washington Irving, was called the most beautifully gotten up book
that had appeared here up to then, with its illustrations by
Darley, William Hart, and others, with the engraving by
Richardson. Darley was the sole illustrator of the "Knickerbocker History."

On page 148 of "American Graphic Art," Weitenkampf
tells us that engraving was the principal reproductive medium through which any graphic art was brought before the
public. Book illustration was very popular then—school
books, magazines, comic papers, sometimes an occasional
picture, as for instance, in the Herald of New York. Books
of travel were in much demand, with plenty of pictures in
them. The steel engravings lasted until the Civil War. Darley so illustrated Dickens works, issued by Houghton and
Mifflin. On page 207 of this book of Weitenkampf mentions
the rather mechanical plates after the pictures by Alonzo
Chappell, for, "National Portrait Gallery of Eminent Americans," published by Johnson Fry and Company. Chappell
collaborated with Darley in the illustrations of the Stratford
Edition of Shakespeare, edited by William Cullen Bryant
(1886). That was the last important work of Chappell or
Darley. There was some use for lithography for book illustration—frequently in the 1830's, and it appears in black
and white, in tints, and in full color. Darley's, "Scenes in
Indian Life" (1843), and his illustrations for, "Rip Van
Winkle" (1848)—American Art Union, re-issued much re-
duced, in London, 1850, in six etchings on steel by Charles
Simmes—"Legend of Sleepy Hollow" (American Art Union)
1849; Judd's, "Margaret," (1856), all in outline etched on
stone.

On pages 209-211, Weitenkampf tells us, in the early

Forties', appeared "on the scene, and soon at the front, one who still stands on our records as perhaps the most noteworthy example, everything considered of an all-around illustrator that we have ever had, Felix O. C. Darley," and the author goes on to extoll Darley's industry, "as great as his facility and versatility," and how for years publishers announced that their new books were, "illustrated by Darley," or, "with designs by Darley," Weitenkampf goes on glowingly, "The swing of his style, his big grasp of both individual action and the movement of groups of bodies give his work a distinction even to-day. They really are illustrations, even if there were faults in drawing there the pictures did not just painfully carry out the text, they illumined it. The characters were human, not glorified heroes and heroines."

We learn that Darley's capacity and industry likened him to Dore. Paul Gustave Dore (1837-1883), was the dynamic French artist, illustrator and engraver, born at Strassbourg. He illuminated so many famous books: "Don Quixote," Poe's Raven," "Paradise Lost," and so on, and so on. Sometimes defective in drawing, nevertheless he made an ideal illustrator, full of life and sympathy for all he saw.

Weitenkampf runs over some of the many works Darley did, ever improving as he went on, as humanity should do, we are told. Here are some of Darley's artistic exploits: "his early Philadelphia Street Scenes—Occasional Comics—Title Designs (as for The Lantern)—the illustrations for Irving's, Knickerbocker History of New York—Poe—Wm. Gillmore Simmes (1806-70) wrote many novels about South Carolina (Guy Rivers)—Stories of Western and Southern Life—Juveniles—Frank Forrester's Sporting Books—Tristram Shandy —Joseph C. Neal's Humor— (Nick of the Woods)—T. B. Thorpe (The Bee Hunter)—Cooper (for whom he illustrated both on wood and on metal—over 500 designs)—Dickens (The Boston Edition, besides the English illustrations "the unsurpassed designs of F. O. C. Darley are added")—Lossing's, Our Country—Evangeline—Shakespeare." And besides all these, there were many bank note vignettes, and the large Civil War framing pictures "March to the Sea"—all meritorous. Is there any wonder that errors would creep in? Or that he should "develop a manner, but at its best, and it was remarkably often at its best. It approached so closely to style as to challenge a definition of difference."

In Darley's preparatory sketches there is so much to charm—so many ideas for later vignettes and interesting examples of how he tried his pencil in making little swirls to get movement, or fix composition—also little sketches from nature to be kept until some time he might need to use them. Always alert, quietly alive, traveling with his eyes and wits, he made an impression on his fellow artists as well as his public, and while not too definite, there was a trend toward imitating him, and not succeeding any too well.

In the 1850's, Harper's was settled as a magazine. At first not too much notice of art was taken there, but gradually the illustrations improved. Among the artists there were: Frank Bellew; J. R. Chapin; Davenport; Darley; Augustus Hoppin (Illustrated "Nothing to Wear," 1859); etc. A number of Harper's artists, at one time or another, were engaged in doing "Comics," Bellew, Darley, Hoppin, E. F. Mullen (one of Artemus Ward's illustrators), etc.

With peace came plenty of good things in the way of art. Appleton's Journal started in 1869 with Winslow Homer, Darley, Frenzeny, and others. Scribner's Magazine started in 1871. Artemus Ward, mentioned above, was the pen name of Charles Farrer Browne (1834-67). He was a newspaper humorist. His Column in the Cleveland Plain Dealer, titled, "Artemus' Sayings," was very popular with its quaint language and uncouth spelling. Winslow Homer (1836-1910) was the artist sent as a special correspondent for Harper's Weekly to report and sketch events in the Civil War. Later, he specialized in marines, landscapes, and genre painting. His picturesque, "Main Coast," and, "The Gulf Stream," are in the Metropolitan Museum in New York. T. H. Matteson was the painter of the, "First Prayer in Congress, "engraved by H. S. Sadd "Matteson had a certain facility which in a greater degree characterized Darley."

Darley's vignette illustrations for Cooper and Dickens were finely reproduced by J. D. Smilie and many others. Page 101, "Darley's remained the most pleasing and satisfactory examples of the employment of steel engravings for book-illustrations." James David Smilie, (1833-1909), was the American engraver and landscape painter. He was the brother of George Henry Smilie who was born in New York City, studied with his father, and did the first work in banknote engraving. He was a founder of the American Water Color Society (1866). He made etchings of paintings by Winslow Homer, Alma Tadema, and others, as well as a number of portraits. Many of his paintings are scenes of the Far West. George Henry Smilie (1840-1921), was the American painter born in New York City, and a pupil of his father, the engraver. Some of his work in the museums are —"The Merrimack River," in the Boston Art Club; "Light and Shadow Along the Shore," in the Union League Club in Philadlephia; "Autumn on the Massachusetts Coast, "Farm Scene," is in the Corcoran Museum. His, "September on the New England Coast," gained a prize at the Exhibit. And then there was Lossing. Benson John Lossing who lived from 1812-1891, was the American illustrator, a wood engraver. Interested in historical matters, he illustrated books on the Revolution and also the Civil War. His birthplace was Beekman, New York. Starting as a farm boy, Lossing became in turn, a watchmaker, whence probably he got his first ideas of engraving, then he worked on a newspaper, and became a good engraver, much interested in history. He illustrated his own works, among them, "History of New York City," (1884); and, "The Empire State," (1887).

The Alma Tadema mentioned a short space back, was the English painter, born in the Netherlands, (Sir) Lawrence, or Laurence Alma Tadema, (1836-1912). His early paintings were of a far-off period of time and place—such as "The Education of the Children of Clovis," (1861). Clovis was the Frankish King, (481-511), and his wife, St. Clotilde. Later he took Egyptian subjects for his paintings, then Greek and Roman. Finally he returned to England, and became a British subject, 1873, and was made a knight in 1899. He was elected a member of the Royal Academy.

And Darley, the Philadelphia boy who once was drawing for Godey's Book had traveled far and wide in the world of Painters and artists, adjusting himself to new ways as he found them out working hard and steadily, learning from all he met with. Only a genius could have kept up his pace. He must have had himself well-disciplined. From his pictures we can see he was sensitive, so truly does he depict emotions, but he made his characters like himself—people who could stand up to life and enjoy it.

In the City Hall of New York City is a portrait of President James Monroe who served from 1817-1825. This portrait was by John Vanderlyn, who was an important painter, doing portraits and historical subjects. John Vanderlyn was born in Kingston, New York, in 1775, and he lived until 1852. Aron Burr helped him to his art education in Paris. Vanderlyn's, "Landing of Columbus," is in the Capitol in Washington. The portrait of President Monroe is in the Mayor's Reception Room at City Hall. In the Board of Estimate Room is a portrait of Henry Clay by John Wesley Jarvis. Henry Clay, the Great Pacificator, Senator from Kentucky, lived from 1777 to 1852. He denounced extremists in the North and South, and upheld the Union.

Neuhaus, in his book, page 62, tells about John Wesley

Jarvis, (1756-1840). He came to New York in 1785. "He dressed like a foreign potentiate, and accompanied by two big dogs, he was a familiar sight on Broadway. He traveled through cities and estates south of Baltimore, and his vogue was as great as Sully." Sully, it will be remembered, was a relative of F. O. C. Darley. New York was described as "divine" by Henry James, on a brief visit here back from England. In City Hall, too, there is a portrait of Stephen Decatur, Commodore of the War of 1812. This portrait is in the Governor's Room and is by Thomas Sully, a connection by marriage with the Darley family.

In the Mayor's Office in City Hall, New York City, is Lafayette's portrait; it hangs over the mantlepiece. This portrait is by Samuel Finley Breese Morse, inventor of the cablegram. In the Museum of the City of New York, is a printed toile handkerchief with vignettes of New York City Street Cries. This was made about 1814. We can read the labels on them, thus "Tea Rusks—hot!," "Bak'd pears," "Strawberries," "Pineapples, Pineapples!" "Hot Corn," "Watermelons," "Here's Milk, Milk!" etc., etc.

All artists worthy of the name must truthfully as possible paint their subjects. Certainly Darley did his best. If it is a portrait to be done, the artist must try to see and bring out the real character of the sitter. Washington was worn out with the number of times he was forced to let himself be put down on canvas. He tried to submit graciously. But after all the great events of his life were over, and he had retired to private life, a certain ennui came over him. He largely lost interest in everyday matters. In 1792, another painter came his way, but this one was welcomed as an old friend, John Trumbull, who had been Washington's Aide-de-Camp in the War. Trumbull was saddened to note the look of age and weariness on the great man's face. This would never do. He must rouse him, Trumbull vowed. So he began talking over old times. Washington, listening, came to—Monmouth, Trenton, Valley Forge—"Princeton!" echoed Washington, and he was back in the keen excitement of those days. "Ah! that's the way I'll paint you!" Trumbull declared, and he did so. And all who knew the Great Chief were struck with Trumbull's finished picture. And like Lafayette, all vowed, "This is our Washington!" This picture is in the New York City Hall, in the Governor's Room.

There is another anecdote indicating the truth as seen by the artist's eye, and this time it is about the great Michelangelo and the "Pieta," now on loan and in public view at the New York World's Fair of 1964. A friend, looking at this piece of sculpture when it was first executed, said critically, "You have made Mary too young looking. You know that Christ was reputed to be from thirty-three to thirty-nine years of age at the time of the Crucifixion." "No," Michelangelo was firm, "No, a good woman stays young much longer than one without virtue." And so, of course, the other had to bow to this direct and telling assertion.

Darley tried to give the facts as he saw them, nothing trivial or weak—neither did he over-glorify his subjects. He was both artist and illustrator, and one of the definitions of illustration, is—*illumination*. That is what he always attempted—illumination—to throw light on his subject—to bring it out in its best form, to make it clearly interesting to the viewers. And he surely succeeded in his attempts. It grew to be a habit with him. Each time he tried to do his best.

CHAPTER VII

War and Peace

PICTORIAL HISTORY of the Civil War in the United States of America by Benson J. Lossing—1866, Philadelphia, George W. Childs, publisher, Southwest corner Sixth and Chestnut Streets, Darley and other illustrators.

In the Preface, the author gives the reason for issuing such a work. If he had his way, he would have liked the whole terrible period buried in oblivion. But that was not possible, for the whole world knew of the dreadful catastrophe, and it is now history, and as such must be recorded, truthfully.

Lossing calls the work a chronicle of events. He believes the War of the Rebellion was "the work of a few ambitious men, who for selfish purposes and without excuse, conspired to overthrow the Republic. He goes on to say that the Union has been preserved, and "its broad mantle of Love and Charity covers all its children within its folds."

The author declares that he availed himself of the help of others, with pen and pencil, acknowledging his indebtedness to Harper's Weekly, and Frank Leslie's Illustrated Newspaper. Lossing says that the engravings, while they adorn the book, have a higher purpose, "confined to the service of illustrating facts." Lossing ends his Preface with grateful thanks to his publisher, Mr. Childs, "for his aid and encouragement." And so begins the Pictorial History of the War of the Rebellion, with the ever-busy Darley as one of the illustrators.

The Frank Leslie extolled by Lossing was an American engineer (1821-1880). His real name was Henry Carter, born in England. He published periodicals of a family type. His artists did valuable work with their illustrations of the Civil War, giving careful, accurate accounts with pen and pencil of what was then happening on the battlefield. His second wife was Miriam Florence (Folline) Leslie, born about 1836, and died in 1914. After her husband's death, she managed the business, a feminist and the author of several books. She is not to be confused with the actress Mrs. Leslie Carter.

Lossing gives thoroughly the history of the Civil War, illustrating anything he could get hold of to dramatize the dreadful struggle—from battle scene to rosette. There is the facsimile of a ten-dollar banknote issued by the Confederate Treasury Department in Richmond, the Capital of the Confederacy. This note reads, "Payable in two years after date." On such notes, in order to prevent counterfeiting, red and blue inks were used. In this book there were portraits galore. Many of the men were evidently young and good-looking, but they disfigured themselves with outlandish whiskers. Perhaps war privations and duties gave no time for shaving. The plain-faced men looked so much better. Also here in this book was printed the Seal of South Carolina with its palmetto tree. The costumes of the ladies worn at the Inaugural Ball were most accurately drawn in the illustrations here, and described in print with their many ruffles and over-skirts and flounces and puffs and embroideries and loops and quillings and ornaments, and the coiffures were adorned with chaplets of ivy and roses, and so on.

Here in this book, chapters begin with pictures around the opening letter, and each chapter ends with a decorated tail-piece significant of the leading matter detailed in that chapter. And poetry is scattered throughout the book, such as:

"Davis answered short and quick,
With mortar, Paxton and petard,
Sumpter is ours and nobody hurt.
We tender Old Abe our Beau-regard."

And William Cullen Bryant's, Call to Arms," appears in
Lossing's Book:—

"Lay down the axe, put by the spade,
Leave in its track the toiling plow;
The rifle and the bayonet blade
For arms like yours were better now.
And let the hands that ply the pen
Quit the light task and learn to wield
The horseman's crooked brand and rein
The charger on the battlefield."

There were maps of fields of operations especially drawn
to aid the reader in following manoeuvres. Here is a picture
of Dorothy Dix, first woman to obtain the sanction of the
War Department, for the organization of military hospitals.
Dorothy Lynch Dix, (1802-87), was born in Worcester, Mass-
asschusetts, and she became a philanthropist, and she secured
many improvements in hospitals and prisons. Picture follows
picture in this book—soldiers' tents in Battery Park, New
York City—Duryea's Zouaves—Lincoln's residence at Springfield—a portrait of old Winfield Scott in 1865, hale and
hearty—the fine group portrait of Lincoln and his Cabinet
—all pictures signed.

Darley would try anything. If given a book or character
or scene, he would study that particular idea until it had
become real and human to him. For example, one of his
pictures is the death of Pere Marquette. Jacques Marquette,
(1637-75), was the French Jesuit missionary. He was sent
to Canada, called, New France, to teach the Indians in 1666,
when he was twenty-nine years old. He soon became a great
favorite with the Indians, a born linguist, he picked up the

90

"WHEN THEY HAD REACHED THE PLACE, THEY FOUND ONLY EMBERS AND ASHES"

(from *Evangeline*, by Longfellow)

Courtesy of the Philadelphia Museum of Art. Photograph
by A. J. Wyatt, staff photographer

language and quickly made himself understood by the red men. Later he opened another mission at Point St. Ignace (near Macinac Island). Then Joliet, the French explorer, arrived here, December 8th, 1672, with orders from the Jesuit authorities to accompany him, and see if he could repeat his success with Indians along this new route. They started out in 1673, and traveled by Green Bay, Fox River, and the Wisconsin. Then, hearing of a great river beyond, he went on with the party and reached the Mississippi. He has been called, the Discoverer of the Mississippi. They proceeded down this to the mouth of the Arkansas, but went no further as the Spaniards below were threatening. They returned by way of Lake Michigan. He promised the Indians he would come back and start a mission for them. But worn out with his labors, he died on the site of Ludington, May 18th, 1675. His diary and maps and records are about the only records we have of the Expedition. His statue, the Discoverer of the Mississippi, has been placed in the Hall of Fame by the State of Wisconsin, in Washington.

Louis Joliet (sometimes spelled with two l's), 1645-1700, was born in Quebec, Canada. He was an adventurous explorer and fur trader. There is a city in Illinois named Joilet, with a well-equipped prison there. The Mississippi River is the greatest river of North America, and has been called, "The Father of Waters." It is two thousand, four hundred and seventy-seven miles long, and the Mississippi-Missouri is the longest water-course in the world. Superlatives are common in this country. The Mississippi is America's prize agricultural section, often menaced by floods.

Of a very different sort from the saintly Father Marquette, is another characer drawn by Darley, for his Shakespeare work, none other than the doughty Falstaff, Shakespeare's greatest comic character. Huge and bluff and swaggering, Shakespeare liked him so well, he had him appear in two of his plays, "Henry IV," and the "Merry Wives of Windsor."

He was the jolly companion to the young Prince Hal, later Henry V, and some say that when Hal assumed the dignity of his kingly office and gave up his riotous companions, especially Falstaff, it broke the old fellow's heart, and some blame Shakespeare here for turning Hal into what some call, a prig. Be that as it may, Falstaff has been called a gentleman, in spite of his follies. How Darley had grown artistically when he got to Shakespeare—a rise in the world from those earlier days of some of the comics. It showed he had not wasted his time. It is said that when Shakespeare found any part of a play, or a character, or some turn of events therein very popular with his audiences, he would take advantage of this good luck, and would repeat it elsewhere and with the same success. He had so much to do, he had to try and save himself as much as possible.

Darley, with mother and father both acting folk, must have liked the theatre. He must have seen Falstaff on the stage—the boaster with his, "Discretion is the better part of valor," a human sort, loving, emotional, perhaps acting a part all the time to bolster new courage. Falstaff was a great creation of Shakespeare's. Did Darley choose this character to illustrate? Or was it simply assigned to him? He did it as if his heart were in the work. But then that was his art, always aiming for the best, unhappy if he could not achieve it.

Alonzo Chappell collaborated with Darley in illustrating the Stratford edition of Shakespeare, this edition edited by William Cullen Bryant. Chappell died in 1890 or 1891, and Darley in 1888. William Cullen Bryant's father was a medical doctor, and as a friend of his, a famous physician by the name of William Cullen, had just died before the boy was born, decided to give this friend's name to the child—hence, William Cullen Bryant, hoping, perhaps, that the boy, too, would become a great physician.

However, as the boy grew and showed a love for poetry,

the father led him along that line and taught him what he could of verse. The boy went for two years to Williams College, and then left to study law. But when he was eighteen years old, he wrote the poem that still lives, "Thanatopsis." He wrote, "To a Waterfowl," when he was twenty. By then he had found out that he did not care for law, but how could one earn a living writing poetry? The poem was sent to the North American Review, then edited by two young men, Richard Henry Dana and Edward Tyrrel Channing, both of these editors to become famous later. They liked the poem, and were curious about the author. Dr. Bryant was then serving in the State Senate, and Dana, hearing there was a Senator Bryant, went to the Massachusetts State Senate, then in session, and asked to have Dr. Bryant pointed out. A tall, middle-aged business type of man was indicated, and Dana, sure that one could not be the poet, left without meeting the Doctor. But the poem was published in the North American Review, and soon afterwards both editors met the real poet and became good friends.

He sent more poems to these editors, and they liked them and him so well, that they invited him to appear before the Phi Beta Kappa Society at Harvard, and for this occasion, he wrote, "The Ages." In 1826, he brought out a small book of verse, and was given a good review by Julian Verplanck, in the New York American. Bryant moved to New York in 1825, after a varied experience with writing. In 1826, he went with the Evening Post, and in 1828, was made chief editor. And there he stayed for a famous career. In 1870-71, he published his translations of the Iliad and the Odyssey. And he kept on writing his worthy poetry to the end. He also had another gift, he could talk very well. He delivered the eulogy for his friend, the painter, Cole, in 1845. He did the same for Cooper, and Irving, and when the statue to Morse was set up in Central Park, he made the address. And when the statues and monuments to Shakespeare, Scott, and

Halleck, were likewise installed in the Park, Bryant's dedicatory speeches were in order. Right up to the busy end of life he kept active, both mentally and physically. He died quickly and quietly, June 12, 1878.

Darley knew Bryant, and he knew Darley—the friends of both were all the artistic set in New York—artists and literary people. Of course Darley was much younger than Bryant, twenty-eight years younger, but he was mature and could appreciate such a friendship. Richard Henry Stoddard (1825-1903) was a friend of both Bryant and Darley. Stoddard was born in Hingham, Massachusetts, with a sea captain for a father. He was a poet and literary editor of the New York World. Then he edited Aldine, a New York art and literary journal. He was literary Editor of the New York Mail And Express until his death in 1903. He wrote a "Life of Washington Irving, and he also wrote about Darley in the National Magazine, September, 1856.

Darley's pictures were substantial, not over-earthly, but real. He saw what other people saw, but more vividly and deeply. He put down what his outward and inward eye saw truthfully, but screened through his own originality. LaFolette's book, page 86, has this to say about other artists and their work—"Leslie complained that Gilbert Stuart's pictures sometimes looked as if one could blow them away—and this stricture applies to many of these pretty pictures."

Among others who illustrated for Harper's Weekly, was J. R. Chapin, and who later illustrated Edgar Fawcett's, "Owen Delaplaine." Edgar Fawcett (1847-1904), was a New York author of poems, plays, and novels. His fiction deals mostly with life in New York, "A Hopeless Case," (1881) and, "New York," a novel, 1898. Chapin started in with Harper's first decade (1851-61). Others around this time working for Harper's were Frank Bellew, J. M. Coffin, W. H. Davenport, Darley of course, Dallas, C. E. Doepler, Hinslie, Hitchcock (the Hitchie of Vedder's Story—Elihu Vedder,

1836-1923), American illustrator and painter. Illustrated, "The Rubyiat." His murals are in the Library of Congress).

Omar Khayyam, born in Persia in the 11th century, was a mathematician and an astronomer. He wrote the "Rubaiyat," which was made into English by Edward FitzGerald, in 1859. This Edward FitzGerald was an English poet, who lived from 1809-83. He made three versions of Omar Khayyam's "Rubaiyat," in 1859, 1868, and 1872. E. H. Winfield has also made a translation of these mystic quatrains. Some believe these short poems were meant by Omar Khayyam to be taken literally, others see veiled meanings in them and haxe likened them to the Song of Solomon. Sufism was a mystic philosophy in the 16th century, particularly strong in Persia. Sufis was a monastic order whose members sought personal union with God. The symbolic Persian poets were Ferid el-Din Attar; Hafiz; Jami, Omar Khayyam.

Augustus Hoppin, mentioned before, the illustrator of "Nothing to Wear," 1854, later illustrated books by W. D. Howells, 1873-1920, born at Martin's Ferry. His father was a country newspaper publisher. William Dean Howells was Consul at Venice from 1861-65. He wrote, "The Wedding Journey," "The Rise of Silas Lapham," "The Coast of Bohemia," and so on, and so on. Hoppin also illustrated Dinah Maria Mullock's, "Tales." This author lived from 1826 to 1870, an English writer, novelist, author of "John Halifaz, Gentleman" (1856). Also Hoppin illustrated for G. W. Curtis. George William Curtis (1824-92), the American author, was at Brook Farm and wrote it up. His "Prue and I," 1856, was perhaps his best known work. He became chief editorial writer for Harper's Weekly. He also conducted, "The Editor's Easy Chair," Department in Harper's Magazine. He spent much of his time lecturing, one of the most popular of a group of lyceum lecturers. He served as Chancellor of New York University. Edward Cary wrote his Life in 1894.

E. F. Mullen was another of the artists and illustrators, also Thomas Thwaites, also H. J. Stephens, and Darley was considered tops as illustrator. People wanted landscape pictures like those they had seen in, "Picturesque America," 1874. On page 89, of the LaFolette Book, reads, "Striking scenes were seized on by painters and re-told by gravers, such as "Plymouth Rock," 1869, by Joseph Anderson; "Lady Washington's Reception Day," after Huntington; and, "On the March to the Sea "after Darley.

Hartman, in his book, "A History of American Art," E. C. Page & Co., Boston, 1911, page 92, declares that," "Before the War (Civil War) illustrated magazines and illustrated books were the exception," and he adds that the "improvement of process work and the development of wood-engraving went hand in hand with this movement up to the time painters were the illustrators and engravers, too." Nast was an artist before he became a cartoonist and caricaturist. Then week after week he would contribute to Harper's Weekly his explosive cartoons concerning Tammany, etc. There was some dispute as to how just some of his work was. Nevertheless no one disputed how powerful it was in arousing the people. Then when the Seventies came along, there were many who could highly please the readers with their sketches. But Darley was greater than most of them. He could indicate character. As said before, he was something like Dore, the celebrated French illustrator and engraver, or the earlier French artist, Honore Daumier, (1808-79), cartoonist and lithographer as well as painter. But Darley's work had more truth and sweetness to it. Daumier's "Good Samaritan," is at the Metropolitan Museum in New York City.

Howard Pyle had something of Darley's charm, but, of course Pyle, was of a later day (1853-90), when art matters were easier and more developed. Pyle's drawings for "Robin Hood," and the Colonial times of New England and New

Amsterdam were great favorites in their day. As the author, Hartman, so well says about Pyle, and the same might have been said of Darley, "He made the strange familiar to us."

In the Eighties, illustrations became commercialized. Most artists would not refuse to do illustrations since they were profitable. Darley, right up to the end, never was neglectful in his work, indeed it seemed to better with the years, as if it were quite true that practice makes perfect. And what stern years of practice he had. As Hartman says, page 110, "As time went on, painters became the illustrators, and a painter is seldom a good illustrator, as most usually lack the true illustrative aptitude." Darley was more than a painter. He was, in truth everything. Hartman says on page 145 of his book, "The most perfect steel engraving for the reproduction of a painting was Asher Durand's rendering of Vanderlyn's "Ariadne." He devoted four years to the work. Another fine steel engraving of that time was Casilear's after Huntington's "Sybil." John William Casilaer (1811-93) was an American engraver and landscape painter. Steel engraving was replaced by revived wood-engraving, when the important magazines began to be illustrated, but this period only lasted about 1878 to 1894. Then modern methods took over.

William James Linton (1812-97) came over from England in 1867, and helped revive the art of wood-engraving. This artist and political reformer illustrated William Cullen Bryant's "The Flood of Years." Frederick Juengling (1824-69) came to America from Germany in 1866 and set up an engraving firm in New York in 1867. One of his best etchings was, "Porrtait of J. McNeil Whistler," after Whistler's painting.

Then photography took over. Hartman says, page 151, "There is no reason why a photographer should not do as individual work as an artist in other black and white mediums." And this author goes on to ask, "What differentiates a genius from the ordinary being and lifts him above the multitude?" And he answers this with, "To me it is the mastery of three gifts—which others also possess, yet not to the same degree and not united, namely: first, the power of selection, in which technical accomplishments find their expression—second, the depth of emotion which formulates the conception of the idea to be portrayed; and third, perseverance, largely dependent on temperament and constitution."

It was Stieglitz whom all honor directly or indirectly for his photographic work. He was the artistic pioneer and promoted photography to a fine art. Alfred Stieglitz (1864-1946), Steichen came later. Edward Steichen, (born in 1879), is the photographer and painter. His early paintings are in the New York Metropolitan Museum. During World War II, he commanded the U.S. Navy Photographic Department. He is the brother-in-law of the poet, Carl Sandburg.

In 1810, John Trumbull told John Frazee, a stonecutter, that "Sculptors would not be wanted here in America for a century." The ship carvers were the first to do any such work in the figure heads for the ships. Indians and naval heroes were their models.

Hiram Powers (1803-1873), was the foremost American sculptor. He went out to Cincinnati, and while there, he would visit the studio of a German artist with whom he had struck up an acquaintance. He learned something about modeling, and secured employment in the wax work department of a Western museum. And here some of his illustrations of Dante's Inferno," attracted attention. In 1837, he went to Italy and there developed brilliantly. His famous Greek Slave is in the Corcoran Art Gallery in Washington, done when the Greeks were struggling with the Turks for their freedom. His "California" is at the Metropolitan Museum in New York. Harriet Hosmer of St. Louis, was about our first woman sculptor. The World's Fair gave an impetus to sculpture.

On page 43 of his book, Hartman writes: "I do not think an artist can be too conscientious,' remarked Mr. Augustus St. Gaudens to me one afternoon in his studio.' " That surely went for Darley, too. Augustus Saint Gaudens 1848-1907 was the chief sculptor of his day. Born in Dublin, his chief statue is that of General Sherman at the entrance to Central Park. It is said his "Diana" for the old Madison Square Garden did not please him, so he had it taken down, remodeled and recast at his own expense. He made modern dress decorative in his statuary. Hartman says, "The Relief he made of Robert Louis Stevenson is a poem of lines that express sincerity and artistic achievement, a mixture of idealism and realism which is thoroughly original and speaks a language of its own." St. Gaudens' brother, Louis, 1854-1913, was also a sculptor. Hartman declares on page 90, that "the beauty of our American women has not been glorified half enough by our artists."

A pupil of St. Gaudens was MacMonnies, who was born in Brooklyn, 1863. He was famous for the Fountain at the World's Fair in 1893. His statue, "Civic Virtue," one time in City Hall, caused much controversy. He died in 1937.

Darley was a contemporary of all these people, at least a part of his life and a part of their lives. A largely self-taught artist, he is still alive, while many who achieved fame during his time, are now forgotten. Most of the museums and libraries have drawings and pictures of his. It would be interesting if some time an exhibition of his work could be shown. The public would like it today as much at it did in the past. As the old saying goes, "The artist dies, but his work lives on." How many of the artists and engravers who worked with him in the old days are remembered now? Not a line is given many of them in any encyclopedia. But every well written book of American Art, from his own period up to the present, lauds his work. It was unique.

Of course, it is great to be alive at any time. But somehow, from around 1845 to 1875 or 80, in this country, it must have been an extra great time with so many happenings and an enormous group of vivid characters all about. Dickens visited us here twice in that era—first in 1842, and then wrote scoffingly about Americans. But, later, he came to us, an older and wiser man, in 1867-68, and found us much nicer, but he wore himself out in his readings here to wildly enthusiastic audiences. And Darley illustrated the works of this master of fiction in a masterly way. These illustrations must have pleased Dickens. There were any number of intelligent youngish men eagerly on the go around here in New York then, and its environs.

Albert Brisbane, the social reformer, born in Germany; Horace Greeley, the newspaper man; Nathaniel Parker Willis, the journalist; Donald Grant Mitchell, "Ik Marvel," the author whose works were illustrated by Darley; George Bancroft, the historian; and, of course, "Raymond of the Times," The Times, for the New Year, 1852, had a special eight-page issue with Longfellow's Midnight "Mass for the Dying Year."

Darley was right there, working and mixing in with the active life, always with the shadow of slavery and possible war creeping over what might have been clear bright skies. And then the dreadful catastrophe followed by rainbow years so long awaited and eagerly greeted. There were famous visitors here, too, besides Dickens, Thackeray came to the United States in 1852, and again in 1855, on lecture tours. The Hungarian patriot Louis Kossuth, was another visitor, and in 1852, the Press gave him a dinner at the Astor Hotel which was attended by many famed ones. A little earlier, Mrs. Trollope, in 1832, the English authoress, after traveling all over the United States, went home and harshly criticized the people here, in her "Domestic Manners of the Americans." The Prince of Wales, later Edward VII, was a notable visitor to this country. More and more Americans began taking trips abroad. Darley's deferred journey through the interesting parts of Europe, proved profitable as well as enjoyable, and as has been told before, he set down his experiences in his little journal, "Sketches with Pen and Pencil."

The newspapers were then flourishing and cheap. With excellent editors and writers, much was accomplished in training the taste of the people, as well as giving them the news, for which the American public is always so eager. The Times ridiculed hoop skirts, and called the ailanthus tree, "a filthy foreigner." But this Tree of Life, as it has been called, is still with us, wherever there is still a backyard.

The Tribune under Horace Greeley is said to have been very popular in the West, and Greeley is supposed to have uttered the famous phrase, "Go West, young man!" Horace Greeley was for prohibition, abolition, and against capital punishment. He also backed Dr. Graham (graham bread) who wanted everyone to stop eating white bread, and eat, instead, whole wheat bread, vegetables and fruits. The Tribune was a Republican paper, as it still is.

The Herald, the New York Herald, at first was considered sensational and vulgar. In 1835, James Gordon Bennett, a Scotsman, founded it. He lived from 1795 to 1872. Sometimes the Herald employed illustrators, and Darley got in on this. In 1867, James Gordon Bennett, the son, took over the management of the paper. His life span was from 1841 to 1918. The Tribune financed Stanley's trip to darkest Africa to find the missing missionary, David Livingstone.

It would seem, too, that through the period, 1845 to 1875, this country endured the worst kind of weather. The summers were the hottest, the winters the coldest, and the

101

snows the highest. Perhaps the Weather Bureau then was in its infancy and did not register or report correctly. And some of those extremes must have lingered into the 1880's, when the Big Blizzard of 1888 piled up and put the metropolitan district completely out of control, buried under mountains of snow. Perhaps the central heating now has something to do with the moderation of weather, and winter's chill. Certainly air-conditioning has rendered summer's heat nil, even in the dogdays of July and August.

Another man of Darley's time was Rufus Wilmot Griswold, born in Bennington, Vermont, in 1815, he became the editor of the International Magazine which afterwards was incorporated with Harper's Magazine. A popular book edited by him was "Poets and Poetry of America," (1842), and its companion book, equally popular, "Prose Writers of America, (1846). He edited the first American edition of Milton's prose. He also did a three-volume edition of Poe's works, (1850), and wrote as a preface, "A Life of Edgar Allan Poe," that was harshly criticized. His son, W. M. Griswold, edited his correspondence in 1898.

Edmund Clarence Stedman, 1833 to 1908, was a prominent man in New York, both before and after the Civil War. Besides being in the financial turmoil of Wall Street, he was a poet and a critic, and he also completed some interesting anthologies. He was war correspondent at Washington, 1861-1862, acting for the New York World.

Edwin Forrest, 1806 to 1872, was the famous actor of those days, a tragedian playing in Othello, Macbeth, Iago, and Hamlet. Much rivalry existed between Forrest, the American, and the British tragedian, Macreedy, and when the latter came to act in America, matters flared up into a riot, the Astor Place Riot (1849). Macreedy left the United States, but Forrest went on to well-deserved popularity.

There were many good players then, Edwin Booth, of course, 1833-1893. Laura Keene (1826-1873), was playing in

"Our American Cousins" at Ford's Theatre in Washington when Lincoln was shot there in his box at the theatre. Charlotte Cushman (1816-1876), made her debut as "Lady Macbeth," in New Orleans in 1835. Then came Dion Boucicault (1822-1890), a British actor and playwright. He was in America after 1853. His famous plays and adaptations were many, and among them were: "The Colleen Bawn," 1862; "Rip Van Winkle," 1867; and "The Octoroon," 1859.

The New York Sun was at first a paper for the poorer classes, but after Dana became Editor, the paper attained a very high standard. Charles Anderson Dana, (1819-97), was at one time a member of the Brook Farm group. He went with the Tribune in 1847. In 1863-64, he became Assistant-Secretary of War. In 1868, he was made Editor of the Sun, and after that, both he and the paper became famous, "Dana of the New York Sun." Francis Browne in his book, "Raymond of the Times," page 18, calls the New York Evening Post, of that time, "dignified," with the poet, William Cullen Bryant, as Editor. It was a flourishing time for newspapers, so many people were able to read them. On page 61 of Browne's book, "Raymond of the New York Times," quotes Horace Greeley as saying, "New York has become (1839) the Metropolis in our country, not only commercially, but in literature and the arts." Nor was this country's growth without humanitarian issues. Henry Bergh, (1820-88), organized The Society for Prevention of Cruelty to Children, and he also started the Society of Prevention of Cruelty to Animals. Elizabeth Blackwell, (1821-1910), was the first woman physician in this Country. She was brought from England, in 1832. Later she taught school and studied medicine privately, finding it difficult to be admitted to a medical College because she was a woman. Finally the Medical School at Geneva, New York, admitted her, and she gained a degree of M.D. in 1849. In 1854, she helped organize the infirmary for Women and Children. Her war work was very

103

helpful, in organizing the Women's Relief Association for sending supplies and nurses to the War Front. Peter Cooper was a man who did much for the world in general and New York in particular. He was born in 1791 and lived until 1883. A man of wealth, he interested himself in many things. He built the first locomotive in America, a small experimental engine for the B. & O. Railroad. Later he gave much assistance to the laying of the first Trans-Atlantic Cable. His best known gift was the Cooper Union for the advancement of science and art, 1853, with free tuition in art, science, and technology.

The Great Eastern, that tremendous craft, in 1868, attempted to lay the Atlantic Cable, but the cable parted. However, later on, with a new cable, all went well, and since then a number of cable companies were formed.

THE VILLAGE BLACKSMITH, BY LONGFELLOW

Courtesy of the N. Y. Public Library, Prints Division

CHAPTER VIII

A Young World

JOHN FRAZEE (1790-1852), was a pioneer sculptor who made busts of Daniel Webster and John Marshall, Chief Justice of the Supreme Court, (1801-35). Frazee was the first to make a bust here in marble, of John Weeks, in 1824. About 1875, municipal monuments began to be erected in great quantities, most of them worthless as art. H. K. Browne was the sculptor of the General Washington Statue on Union Square, New York, called the best equestrian statue in America.

John Rogers (1829-1904), was the American sculptor who made the "Slave Auction," used by the Abolitionists for propaganda. The Rogers groups were manufactured in great quantities by machines and sold cheaply to adorn modest homes.

The first book or magazine illustrations in this country were of a comic nature—cartoons or caricatures. The word, caricature, is from the French and Italian "Caricature—Caricare"—meaning to charge, over-charge, exaggerate. Webster's Dictionary defines, "caricature—1. Grotesque or ludicrous—exaggerated, or distorted by exaggeration. 2. A picture, a description, etc. characterized by burlesque exaggeration or distortion. And a cartoon is a pictorial caricature.

Darley's only professional early work was a series of scenes in Indian Life with much that was serious in these illustrations. However, he did make illustrations for the Literary American Humorous Works. He was clever, indeed, and he was quick to seize upon any slight twist away from the normal, and make that trait laughably observed.

In the early days, painters usually did any work when it was needed. Later Darley greatly pleased Irving, with his illustrations for "Rip Van Winkle," and "The Legend of Sleepy Hollow," and here Darley exhibits some slight caricature, but his humor was in such good taste, it was an art in itself. Then followed Darley's successful flow of illustrations for all the important authors of his own day—and earlier.

John LaFarge, the painter, born, 1835 and died, 1910, did illustration work, also, of high merit. There was his, Tennysons's, "Enoch Arden," and he illustrated "Songs of the Old Dramatists," and, "Songs of Feeling and Thought."

Darley did beautiful illustrations for Laurence Sterne's "Tristram Shandy," "Longfellow's Poems," "Dickens' Works." His illustrations in collaboration with Alonzo Chappel in Shakespeare's works were exceptionally fine. The Complete Works of Shakespeare, edited by William Cullen Bryant, contained one hundred photo-gravure illustrations from original drawings by Darley and Chappell.

Darley could do ghosts very well, as is shown here in the play of Julius Caesar. Brutus, alone and unable to sleep, stirred earlier against Caesar, calls out to his page, to bring a light to dispel the fantasies his troubled brain has imagined. "Get me a taper in my study, Lucius," Brutus is deep in awful thoughts, and in a haze, the ghost is seen before him. And likewise in Hamlet, his father's ghost appears before Hamlet.

Bryant, the editor, commenting on "Anthony and Cleopatra," says, "This tragedy was first printed in the Folio of 1623." Here Bryant quotes Coleridge who said, "This play of Anthony and Cleopatra should be perused in mental contrast with Romeo and Juliet as the love of passion and appetite opposed to the love of affection and instinct."

106

Bryant remarks of Laertes, in the play of Hamlet, is "A good portrait of a weak nonentity." And Bryant goes on to say that the part of Laertes was often taken by John McCullough in his early days. John McCullough, (1837-85), was the American actor given to tragic parts. He was born in Londonderry, Ireland. In 1866-68 he acted with Edwin Forrest. Bryant also gives the information that "Opelia," was the part in which Peg Woffington won her first fame. Peg Woffington—Margaret Woffington, (1714-1760) was also in the part of "Cordelia," in King Lear, and King Lear is illustrated both by Chappell, plate I, and by Darley, plate II, Act III, Scene II—Lear out on the heath in a raging storm, and his fool with him. Bryant comments on these two illustrations of the same scene. He writes, "It is interesting to note how differently and yet with how great a purity of vigor and genuine feeling, the same scene has been treated by Mr. F. O. C. Darley and by Mr. Alonzo Chappell. The figure of Lear in Mr. Darley's picture, like that in Mr. Chappell's, is full of life and intensity, the face being strong and noble through all its wild insanity. His utter oblivion to ought except his sorrow and his wrongs, his defiance, indeed, of the elements forms an admirable contrast to the poor fool who feels the pelting rain drenching him to his very bones, and would fain seek shelter for the material man even though his soul is occupied with concern for his loved and grief-stricken master." This passage, in which Lear appears as illustrated, contains the famous lines:

Lear:
>Blow, winds, and crack your cheeks!
>>rage; blow!
>You cataracts and hurricanes, spout
>Till you have drenched our steeples;
>>drowned the cocks!
>You sulphurus and thought-exciting fires,
>Vaunt couriers of oak-cleaving thunder-bolts

Strike flat the thick rotundity o' the world,
Singe my white head! And then, all-shaking thunder
Crack nature's molds, all germans spill at once,
That make ingrateful man!"

Edwin Booth played Romeo on the opening of his new theatre in New York, February 3, 1869.

These two eminent artists, Darley and Chappell, went through the entire list of Shakespeare's plays, giving exact and beautiful illustrations of the great words spoken by the great characters that Shakespeare made come alive and live immortally. Darley also illustrated the other Shakespeare edition in his own inimitable way. All the best artists tried doing these pictures, mostly caricatures. Among these were Homer Davenport, Brush, and Powers.

The founder of the Boy Scouts, Daniel Carter Beard, 1850-1941, was also a naturalist and an illustrator. Paul Frenzenczy, Hopkins, etc. Edwin Abbey was another illustrator as well as a painter (1852-1911). He illustrated Herrick's poems; Goldsmith's, "She Stoops to Conquer," and the Shakespeare Comedies. Poe's works were favorites with the illustrators. Well-made books demanded fine illustrations. Gift books were such, made for all degrees, and for all purses, but not all of the same high quality.

Darley was thoroughly an American, proud of being a citizen of the United States. He was born in conservative Philadelphia, and he grew up in the traditions of this Country. He was truly an American artist and could depict so well the varied aspects of this golden continent. His eye was quick and his mind was quick, and he could estimate the different groups of people he knew and traveled among. That was how he came to be so successful, as an illustrator. And he was able to transfer his thoughts and inferences with the aid of his pen or pencil or brush to paper or board or canvas in a truthful and interesting style, that made critics and the public approve. Consequently his gifts were in much demand. But he was more than an American, he was a man of the world. He would appreciate the background of culture in the old world whence our pioneers had come. He read, he studied, he took part in everything going on about him, that was worthwhile.

From his mother and father, both English actors who came and settled here, Darley certainly got his dramatic sense. He knew how to stage groups in his pictures, how to depict emotion, how to bring humor in if needed—and all with clean, definite strokes that spoke of genius. He reached out on every hand for more knowledge, more opportunity, in an effort to improve himself and his work. When he was able to, he went abroad, and traveled through charming places he had heard of and where he had friends. And he was welcomed and made much of all over. And after he returned, he set down his impressions in a simple and delightful way in a little book. He enjoyed life and all it brought him. He was a genuine artist, a hard and conscientious worker, never getting into a rut, but always trying for better things, willing to struggle and fail in an attempt rather than not try.

James Thomas Flexner, in his book, "American Painting," declares, "The panorama of American painting is a panorama of American life." Washington Allston, the first authentic American painter, went to England in 1801. There he met Coleridge who had been collaborating with Wordsworth in Lyrical Ballads, the beginning of the Romantic movement. Coleridge was so impressed by Allston that he declared the Americans alone seemed able to represent nature, correctly, "not the dead shapes, the outward letter, but the life of nature revealing itself in the phenomenon."

When one thinks of Fenimore Cooper, one thinks of Darley's illustrations. Some believe they made Cooper. In "The Shock of Recognition," edited by Edmund Wilson,

1943, New York, Doubleday, Doran and Company, Inc.—there are two essays concerning Cooper's writings. A very humorous one by Mark Twain, called, "Fenimore Cooper's Literary Offenses." There is so much Twain does not like about Cooper, and he scolds Professor Lounsbury (1833-1915) who calls Cooper's writings, "all words of art." Thomas Reynesford Lounsbury was long time a professor of English at the Yale Sheffield Scientific School. Mark Twain rails also against Brander Matthews, in as much as he says "Natty Bumpo is one of the very greatest characters in fiction." Brander Matthews (1852-1929) graduated from Columbia College, and became Professor of Dramatic Literature at Columbia in 1900, and remained, in this post until his retirement in 1924. Mark Twain likewise in his essay, belays Wilkie Collins because of his declaration that, "Cooper is the greatest artist in the domain of romantic fiction yet produced by America." William Wilkie Collins, (1824-89), born in London, was the son of William Collins, the painter. Wilkie Collins was a novelist, known especially for his, "Woman in White" (1860); and "The Moonstone" (1868). He was associated with Dickens in literary work. Mark Twain objects in facetious manner to Cooper's stories in eighteen points, such as his way of telling them; the language used; the characters; and so on and so on. Among these points, Mark Twain insists that, "A tale shall accomplish something, and arrive somewhere," but Cooper's Tales fill neither of these requirements." He accuses Cooper of small invention, declaring he had a few tricks he worked over and over again, one was *a dry twig*. "Every time silence is worth four dollars a minute," someone steps on a dry twig, and *crash;* alarm begins to spread. In fact, Mark Twain asserts "The Leather Stocking Series," should have been titled, "The Broken Twig Series." He says that Cooper was not a word musician. In Twain's belief, those professors who praised Cooper's works should have read some of them.

Edmund Wilson, the Editor of "The Shock of Recognition," was born in 1895, an American writer and critic. He also wrote plays, poems, stories, and novels. Edmund Wilson, commenting on Mark Twain's criticism of Cooper's writings, tells that this piece by Twain first appeared in the North American Review, July, 1895. And Wilson notes that Frank Norris, in "Responsibilities of a Novelist," 1903, also belittles Cooper, declaring that although Cooper was an American, he is a direct follower of the English Romantics, and that his Indians act like Byron's, and orate as if they were in the pages of Walter Scott.

But Wilson himself feels that these critics do not quite understand Cooper, nor do they comprehend "The Leather Stocking Tales." Such are not realistic stories, nor are they meant to be so, but rather romantic myths. He admits that Cooper may have written in a clumsy way, but he says, "There is always a poet present to relieve the abominable craftsmanship." And Wilson quotes from Cooper his description of Glimmerglass Lake, "as limpid as pure air," and so on. Wilson calls his own book, "The Shock of Recognition," and goes on to explain the title—This title is from a line in Melville's poem, and it means the shock occurs, "when the very good writer is confronted by the very bad."

In Wilson's book, there is a piece by D. H. Lawrence on Fenimore Cooper's Leather Stocking Novels. David Herbert Lawrence, (1885-1930), the English novelist, likes Cooper's stories, and says he loved the Leather Stocking Tales, and he names Cooper as, "first, an artist; then, an American, then, a gentleman." Lawrence thinks the Leather Stocking Tales form a sort of American Odyssey, with Natty Bumpo an Odysseus. He feels that Cooper dreamed the nucleus of a new society. "These novels go backwards from old age to golden youth." That is America. It starts very old, and and gradually sloughs off the old skin to a new youth. The pictures Cooper drew in words in the Leather Stocking Tales,

111

and illustrated by Darley, Lawrence declares, "are the love-liest pictures in all literature"—the village street, the Indians, the Christmas time, and then, Spring, with its vernal freshness, the myriads of birds, night fishing on the lake—as Lawrence says, "Cooper was writing at a safe distance, and so he could idealize."

The Frank Norris, mentioned earlier, was the American novelist, who lived from 1870 to 1902. He was born in Chicago. He did newspaper work in San Francisco. His novel, the "Octopus," (1901), Then, "The Pit" was published in 1903. "The Wolf" was never published, nor completed.

Cooper's Novels, in thirty-two volumes, illustrated by F. O. C. Darley, is considered one of the best editions, and later sets with Darley's illustrations, were based on this earlier set. The Household edition of J. Fenimore Cooper's works in twelve volumes (Hurd & Houghton, and, later Houghton Mifflin, 1876-1884), have prefaces by Susan Fenimore Cooper, the novelist's daughter. Then there was the Mohawk edition, New York, Putnam's (1895-1900), which includes Ned Meyer. We always think of Cooper as a New Yorker, as a matter of fact, he was born in Burlington, New Jersey, but taken the next year with the rest of the family, by his father, to Otsego Lake, New York, starting the village of Cooperstown. Some of Cooper's critics believed him incapable of depicting a woman, but Griswold, in his "Prose Writers" rejects this idea, by citing "Maud Meredith," as among the first-class portraitures. "Ned Meyers" is a biography.

Nearly all of Cooper's books were translated into all or almost all of the European languages. Some critics insist his leading characters were all too much alike. Cooper was the first American novelist to be recognized in a world-wide fashion. Darley was commissioned to illustrate Cooper's works for James G. Gregory. These illustrations were steel engravings, also published as the Cooper Vignettes," 1862.

Alexander Hay Ritchie, the engraver and painter, as noted before, engraved some of Darley's historical pictures: "The First Blow for Liberty," (Battle at Concord Bridge) "Nathan Hale's Last Words"; "Washington's Entry Into New York."

S. B. Morse became acquainted with Daguerre and they remained good friends. Daguerre was elected an honorary member of the National Academy of Design, proposed by Morse. Louis Jacques Mande Daguerre, (1789-1851) was the French scene painter who invented the daguerreotype, the forerunner of the photograph. Morse with Professor John Draper, took the first daguerreotype to be seen in this country. This art became very popular. (S. F. B. Morse, 1791-1872).

In Wilson's Business Directory, 1872-73, there were over one hundred and fifty dealers advertising under "photographs," although in the index to this book, the listing was under "Daguerrerotype Apparatus," and "Daguerreotype Likenesses."

Darley's "Composition in Outlines" from Hawthorne's "Scarlet Letter" 1871, was a series he dedicated to Longfellow. Nathaniel Hawthorne, (1804-64), was born in Salem, Massachusetts. He attended Bowdoin College where he was a classmate of Longfellow. His "Twice Told Tales" (1837), and the second series, 1842, received plenty of notice. He tried the Brook Farm experiment, but gave it up. In 1842, came his, "Moses from an Old Manse," and then the dark, brooding, "Scarlet Letter" (1850). The "House of the Seven Gables" (1857), his "Wonder Book and Tanglewood Tales" are children's stories.

D. H. Lawrence, in Wilson's book "The Shock of Recognition," calls "The Scarlet Letter" an allegory. Sin is shown not as the breaking of Divine Commands, but as the breaking of one's own integrity. There is a dark Puritan atmosphere to this book. But Darley could not illustrate it that way. With actors for mother and father, he was not a puritan. He was an American—not a part of that dark evil that came across the water to America. Darley made the story human, as all his pictures are. Hawthorne's "Blithedale Romance," is based on the Brook Farm experiment, that Utopia where all the broad-minded people there got sick of each other, and it is said, fought like cats and dogs until the whole thing went to pieces. Lawrence, like most critics, thinks Hawthorne a "strange man with deep convictions, but he can write well, and he gave some lovely settings."

Earlier it was noted that Brutus proved a good model for Darley in his illustrations for the play of "Julius Caesar." A part of this striking scene is given below:

ACT II, SCENE I—JULIUS CAESAR—SHAKESPEARE

Brutus
>   I cannot by the progress of the stars,
>   Give guess how near to day,—Lucius, I say!
>   I would it were my fault to sleep so soundly.
>   Ho, Lucius, wheu! Awake, I say!, What, Lucius!

Enter Lucius
>   Called you, my Lord?

Brutus
>   Get me a taper in my study, Lucius!
>   When it is lighted come and call me here.

Lucius
>   I will, my Lord.

Brutus (musing)
>   It must be by his death; and, for my part,
>   I know no personal cause to spurn at him,—

But for the general. He would be crowned,
How that might change his nature, there's the question:
It is the bright day that brings forth the adder;
And that craves wary walking. Crown him?—
        that—
And then, I grant, we put a sting in him,
That at his will he may do danger with.
The abuse of greatness is when it disjoins
Remorse from power: and, to speak truth of
        Caesar,
I have not known when his affections swayed
More than his reason. But 'tis a common proof
That lowliness is young ambition's ladder,
Whereto the climber-upward turns his face;
But then unto the ladder turns his back,
Looks in the clouds, scorning the base degrees
By which he did ascend. So Caesar may;
Then, lest he may, prevent. And, since the quarrel
Will bear no color for the thing he is,
Fashion it thus; that what he is, augmented,
Would run to these and these extremities:
And therefore think him as a serpent's egg,
Which, hatched, would as his kind grow mischievous:
And kill him in the shell."

In Wilson's book, Edgar Allan Poe, writing of Hawthorne, does not consider him original but "peculiar." And Poe holds it is false to believe that, "allegory can be made to enforce truth." Of course, Poe is writing this essay in 1847 and he does not speak or even know yet of The Scarlet Letter of 1850.

Herman Melville in Wilson's book, writes of Hawthorne and His Mosses (1850), that no great writer ever came up to the ideas of his readers. And he reminds us that how few of the Jewish eye-witnesses saw "Heaven in Christ's glance." Melville tells that he was induced to read Hawthorne's "Mosses from an Old Manse" and was transported with delight. But he wonders, is that other side of Hawthorne, the dark side, deliberately darkened to secure better effect for

115

the light side? Melville says he has been chided for speaking of Hawthorne and Shakespeare on the same page. But Melville admits that Hawthorne is not as great as Shakespeare but Herman Melville vows that give the world time and even Shakespeare will be surpassed. This is not an aging world, says Melville, it is as young as when created. He holds that American writers are increasing in greatness. "For genius, all over the world stands hand in hand and one shock of recognition runs the whole circle round." Melville says he was not attempting to write about Hawthorne's "Twice Told Tales," or "The Scarlet Letter," for they are full of such strange beauties, time would fail him. And he further declares that if such stories had been written in England a century earlier than they were, the status of many very important authors would have slipped down, down. And he says further, that as all great portrait painters put something of their own images in these portraits; so do the authors somehow give a true picture of themselves. And he was sure that after reading Hawthorne's works, he had a true picture of him, even though they had never met.

Herman Melville (1819-91). The famous work of this American writer is "Moby Dick, the Whale" (1851). "Billy Bud" is another, not published until 1924. He was born in New York. In 1841 he shipped from New York and spent eighteen months aboard a whaler in the Pacific. He wrote fine Civil War lyrics (1866) and good romantic stories.

Henry James has his say, too, about Hawthorne, and Wilson has repeated it in his book. Henry James (1843-1916), came of a fine old American family. He studied law at Harvard, and then decided to devote himself to writing. So he went to England in 1876, and was well received. In 1915, during World War I he became a British citizen. Everyone knows his "Turn of the Screw," and "Daisy Miller," "Washington Square," "A Passionate Pilgrim," and many others. However, he did like Americans. In his writings, he owes much to Hawthorne. James was of Irish stock, and he seemed more like a New Englander than a New Yorker, with much puritan, reformatory and moral preoccupations which he caught from Hawthorne. It is difficult to understand James' infatuation with England. But, of course, when you are welcomed, you grow to love the people who make you feel so much at home. Henry James considered Hawthorne the most valuable man of letters that America has produced. James comments thus: "Hawthorne was so modest and his literary output so small, it seems almost an injustice to speak of him in the same breath with American success and opulence." But, then, admits James, "It takes time for literature to flourish in any civilization. America is still a new country. In his own way he was light and dark, shadow and sunshine, he makes New England real though remote, fascinating though fearful. He was born on the 4th of July, 1804." Henry James inserts a little notice that the biography of Hawthorne was given him by George Parsons Lathrop, whose wife was Rose Hawthorne Lathrop, Nathaniel Hawthorne's daughter. She became converted to the Catholic faith, and later founded a sisterhood to care for the cancerous poor.

Hawthorne's forebears followed the sea, and some of its mystery must have come down to him, and salted his stories. Henry James says, "The very air of America looks new and young, and the sun seems so fresh and innocent. The past attracts little attention there." Hawthorne himself declares there is little in the physical aspects of Salem to be sentimental about. Hawthorne was not sociable. He liked solitude. Henry James recalls a French critic's remarks in Revue des deux Mondes, 1863, declaring Hawthorne's writings as "fatalistic." James denies this, declaring that Hawthorne was neither morbid nor bitter. It was only his imagination that saw things dark and light. Much of his troubles were due to poverty. "The Scarlet Letter" came out in 1850, and

117

Hawthorne was then forty-six. In 1841 Hawthorne enrolled at the Brook Farm Community. He wrote it up later in his "Blithedale Romance." But the Brook Farm people never recognized it as such. The people there deported themselves well at this Community. James tells us, "No breath of scandal ever rested on them."

"The Scarlet Letter" was written in 1849. The Preface to it is really autobiography with Hawthorne telling of his term of duty in the Custom House. His publisher, James Thomas Fields, (1817-81), was a partner of the firm of Ticknoe & Fields, and published among many others; the works of Emerson, Longfellow, Whittier, etc. Fields published, "Yesterdays with Authors," in which he tells how he went to see Hawthorne when he heard he had been removed from office due to politics. He found Hawthorne very despondent. So Fields urged him to publish something, but Hawthorne said his former work had not proved very popular, and he did not care to try again. But as soon as Fields left the house, Hawthorne came running after him with a roll of manuscript, "The Scarlet Letter." Fields got him to finish the story, and it was published a year later. Henry James tells, that as a child, he was taken to the Annual Exhibition at the National Academy and saw there a picture of Hester Prynne of the Scarlet Letter, a pale woman in a black dress with a scarlet letter on it holding by the hand a little girl. Years later, James tells, when he read the story, it seemed to him he had read it before—but that was because he remembered the picture. James thinks the fault of this book is that the people are not real, there is a cold passionless mood to the story, almost too much atmosphere. James calls Pyncheon in "The House of the Seven Gables," a "masterly picture." Then came "The Blithedale Romance," due to the year at Brook Farm. He bought a little house at Concord. Alcott had lived there, before him. Thoreau told Hawthorne that the house had originally be-

118

longed to a man who thought he was never going to die. But evidently he did, for he was nowhere around. Hawthorne traveled abroad. "Our Old Home, Merry England," he wrote in 1863. It was not too well liked in England. He said the English were thin-skinned. While in Rome he wrote "The Marble Fawn." He came back to America facing hard times and again depression came on him. The Civil War seemed to cast a black shadow over him. He died May 18, 1864. James says "Conscience was his theme." But what is lacking? What makes the stories so grim? "There is a certain misunderstanding. Of course Hawthorne wrote about people with little sympathy." If people failed, oh, how they had to pay for their sins. Expiation was demanded of them, until they were no more. Was reformation impossible? Could they never be received back into the fold? We cannot believe all New Englanders were as stern and cruel-hearted as we have been told. There is Divine Mercy, then, why not human mercy? Puritanism was too tragic to endure.

In Wilson's book, "The Shock of Recognition," T. S. Eliot, in his Essay on Henry James, a part of this is a comparison of James and Hawthorne, and he calls this, The Hawthorne Aspect, meaning the possible influence or the effect of the earlier writer, Hawthorne on James. Eliot seems to think James is better than Hawthorne, "poor" Hawthorne as he keeps calling him. And yet he rates Hawthorne very high. This paper of Eliot's came out in the Little Review, August, 1918. The whole number of this magazine was given up to James who died in 1916. Eliot says in this essay that, "The soil of his (James) origin contributes a flavor discernible after transplantation in his latest fruit." Eliot admits that Hawthorne had what he calls, "a more acute historical sense" than James. Hawthorne knew New England's history and legends away back but James had largely meager surface history of changing New York. Thomas Stearns Eliot was born in St. Louis, Missouri in 1888. He was awarded the Nobel Prize in Literature in 1942.

119

CHAPTER IX

Panorama

DARLEY'S PICTURE titled "George Washington's Triumphs—Entry Into New York, 1783"—shows the great man coming along in stately fashion, on his big white horse with crowds of excited, jubilant people trying to get near him, to touch him for luck probably. He takes it all in easy fashion. He must have known he would win out. He always did.

A story is told of Washington when he was but fourteen years old, but tall and strong as a man. His mother was the second wife of his father. She was left a widow with a brood of children, George the eldest of them. An older step-brother who had lived abroad, offered to get a midshipman's commission in the Royal Navy for young George who was most eager for this. But his mother objected, and begged him to stay at home and help with the younger children. She urged there would be plenty of chances here for a smart lad like him. So she prevailed, and he gave up the idea of the British Navy. This made her very happy, and we can hear her prophesy, "You'll make a name for yourself, some day, George Washington!" And so he did. But, consider what a different world might have opened up if he had left us and gone to serve England.

The capture of Cornwallis made England pretty sure that America could not be overcome by force. On September 3rd, 1783, the Treaty of Peace between Great Britain and this Country was signed at Paris by David Hartley, Esq. on the part of His Britannic Majesty, and by John Adams, Benjamin Franklin, and John Jay, Esq., on the part of this Country. The Treaty was ratified by Congress in January, 1784.

The British officer in charge here at New York had received orders to evacuate the city, but there were delays owing to a number of British refugees who had to be removed. On Tuesday morning, November 25th, Washington with the United States troops under General Knox, and Governor Clinton, escorted by a body of Westchester light horse, advanced into the upper part of the City of New York at one o'clock. The British left and then the Americans marched in. On the following Monday, December 1st, the Governor of New York gave a fine entertainment to the French Minister, the Chevalier de la Luzerne, which Washington attended. The next evening there were fire works set off at the Bowling Green in Broadway.

On December 4th, Washington took farewell of his army. Congress adjourned to Annapolis. On the way there Washington stopped at Philadelphia and left with the Comptroller there an exact account of all his expenses, written out by his own hand. Washington reached Annapolis on December 19, 1783 and there informed Congress he was ready to resign from the army. It was decided this ought to be a public event. Consequently, on December 23rd, Washington appeared before Congress. A great throng had assembled. George Washington in dignified manner read his speech of resignation. General Mifflin, President of Congress, affected, as all present were, replied in accepting this resignation with almost reverential courtesy. The following day, December 24th, the eve of Christmas, Washington returned to his much beloved Mount Vernon with the parting words, "My Country to the protection of God, and to those who have its charge, to Heaven's keeping."

The Appendix to Chapter IX, Volume 2, of "History

of the United States," by J. A. Spencer, has an extract from Watson's "Men and Times of the Revolution." And from this extract, we learn that it was on the 5th of December that the reporter made his way into the House of Lords in London to hear George III acknowledge the free and independent States of America. It was a rainy day we read, and the outward gloom seeped into the big assembly room. On the walls, dull-hued tapestries depicted the Defeat of the Armada. In the great throng there, the reporter tells of noticing West and Copley, the American painters who lived abroad. After a long wait the King entered, dressed in royal robes and he sat down. Then he drew a paper from his pocket and read his speech.

Usually the King spoke well and distinctly, but this day he was agitated. He told how he tried in every way to settle matters over in America, but nothing came of it. And, so, at last, he decided to declare the Colonies—Here he paused, then went on with emotion as he said the words, "Free and independent States." Then he went on to say that he hoped that "Language, interests, and affection would always prove bonds between the two countries."

On the way out, the reporter mentions that he saw again West and Copley, and they seemed well pleased with the turn of events.

So Darley pictured the great triumphal day with George Washington entering New York to a cheering, overjoyed multitude. Even the branches of the trees were filled with agile ones who wanted to be on top and gain a good view of everything. The ladies and gentlemen, safe up on the balcony were just as joyfully welcoming him with their madly waving handkerchiefs.

From Darley's mild and quiet photograph (from Harper's Weekly) that is the frontispiece in this book, it would seem he must do peaceful scenes the best. But, evidently, he was an expert of emotion. He could depict emotion so

well without exaggeration, except when he wanted to caricature and then he really did it, not cruelly, but explicitly,
fun-provokingly.

In the book "I Remember," by J. Henry Harper, Harper
& Brothers Publishers, 1934, this grandson of the founder
of Harper & Brothers, Publishers, gives the information that
he was born the year that firm started, 1850. In writing about
Franklin Square, the old home of the Harpers Publishing
House, we are informed that Franklin Square was not named
after Benjamin Franklin as many suppose but after a pre-
Revolutionary merchant who lived around there. But the
Harpers put up a bust of Benjamin Franklin on the front
of their new place and so Poor Richard had a memorial
there.

Mr. Harper goes on to tell that the place was badly
burned in the big fire of 1853 but was re-built and remained
there until 1923, when it moved to East 33rd Street. As the
grandson remembers the old place, he recalls some of the
great people who used to come there: Thackeray, Dickens,
Black, Mark Twain, and oh, just about everyone who was
top notch in the literary world here and abroad. The House
of Harper became one of the Sights of New York. Mr.
Harper gives an account of the Art Departments and declares the history was "almost synonymous with American
painting and Black and White illustrations." "Here had come
the golden age of wood-engraving." Mr. Harper recounts
that at one time, Harper & Brothers had going five illustrated periodicals: the Magazine, the Weekly, the Round
Table, the Bazaar, and Golf. All the best artists were eager
for commissions to illustrate as they were so well paid for
their work. He tells of the gilding room where pure gold
leaf was used to stamp the title on the book cover and sometimes in de luxe editions all the book edges were burnished
with gold. He tells also of another little room at the top of
the factory where there was a large tub filled with an iridis-

cent liquid that was used to marbleize the end papers in important books.

Mark Twain (Samuel Clemens), 1835-1910, was a well-known figure at Harper & Brothers. He was born in Hannibal, Missouri, and served as a pilot on the Mississippi, whence he got his pen-name, Mark Twain, from the landsman's call, "Mark twain," meaning two fathoms sounded. He wrote, "Innocents Abroad," "The Adventures of Huckleberry Finn," "The Prince and the Pauper," "The Connecticut Yankee in King Arthur's Court," etc.

Nast did such good work in Harper's Weekly during the Civil War that President Lincoln called him "Our best recruiting Sergeant." In 1871 The New York Times and Nast were running a series of cartoons, and the most famous were the cartoons of Tweedle-dum and Tweedle-dee.

William Allen Butler wrote "Nothing to Wear." His father-in-law was Charles H. Marshall, Captain Marshall of the Black Ball Line, later a shipping merchant. William Allen Butler was an admiralty lawyer. Darley liked the quietude of regions away from the city. He must have been happy illustrating Longfellow's works. One shown here, besides the Evangeline pictures, is "The Village Blacksmith." In this one we see the flaming forge, the sounding anvil, the heavy sledge, and in the distance through the open door, we can see the village church where he goes on Sunday and hears the parson pray and preach, and he hears his daughter's voice singing in the village choir. There is the brawny blacksmith with his assistants all busy getting new shoes ready for the big white horse a neighbor has brought in to be shod. And there is the dog, looking on at this necessary process. The horseman is an interesting looking character. He has a newspaper with him and is evidently having his say over the news he holds in his hands. It must be interesting for the others are turned toward him listening, except the fellow engaged with the patient horse's hoof. He is too busy to look up but he appears attentive, too. It seems strange that Darley has never done any sea scenes. Often in New York, that he came to love, here in the Forties and Fifties nearly everyone had some interest in the sea. But he was an artist, drawn to this mecca, New York, by the beginnings of artistic life here and the magazines and newspapers that were starting to encourage artists and their illustrations.

But his English mother and father must have come to this country on one of the old packet ships. The name packet used to be applied only to ships that carried mail, but later they took on passengers as well. And later, Darley's father was with the U. S. Marines. The packet ships had dangerous crossings in those days. One such vessel was caught in a howling storm off the coast of Ireland, and but one passenger was saved and a small part of the crew. This passenger was an invalid who had to be carried aboard the vessel and yet he lived through all the turmoil somehow. There was such loss of life on those voyages that experiments were made towards life-saving apparatus. The first of these was a kind of mattress put out by a dealer in beds and bedding, a Mr. Jackson, in Pearl Street, New York City. This man, an eccentric character, was known as "Moccasin Joe."

It was unusual for newspapers to contain illustrations, but the New York Herald under James Gordon Bennett, now and then, did have pictures and Darley was an important artist there. The first copy of the Herald appeared May 6, 1835. Bennett wanted this paper he said, "for the great masses of the community." As early as December, 1835, the Herald had the lead in publishing wood cuts in illustration. Harper's Weekly, July 10, 1858, devoted its leading artists to the colorful career of James Gordon Bennett.

The Sketch Book of Geoffrey Crayon (as Washington Irving calls himself here), put out in the author's revised edition with drawings by F. O. C. Darley, engraved by Childs, Herrick, etc. published in New York by G. P. Putnam &

Company, 10 Park Place, 1854, is a fine book in every way—the edges of the pages gilded all around, the cover decorated with gold leaf design, all in all considered by Irving a good piece of work. Darley, too, helped make the book, as well as the book helped to make Darley. The copyright was for the earlier edition, 1848. There are twenty illustrations here besides the frontispiece and the picture of Sunnyside, the home of Washington Irving. In this book is the Preface that appeared in the first edition. In this Preface, Irving explains that almost all the papers in the book were written in England while he was staying and traveling there. He did not intend to publish in England as he thought most of these writings would be more interesting and new to Americans than to the English. But as he puts it, "a change in his fortunes," necessitated the need of money and so he submitted his work to the well-known publisher John Murray, called by those who knew him, "the Prince of Booksellers." Irving laid his cards before Murray but this one was reluctant to attempt the publication but said he would do all he could to help. Irving then considered the Edinburgh publisher Archibald Constable. But before trying Constable, Irving determined to see what help he could get from Walter Scott (not yet Sir Walter Scott). So he forwarded the manuscript of the Sketch Book to him asking if Scott thought these papers "would bear European publication." He had previously been very cordially received at Scott's home in Abbotsford, a few years before.

Scott was greatly taken with the Sketch Book when he saw it and understanding Irving was in need of funds, suggested he take a place as editor of a new periodical that would soon appear under excellent guidance. But steady work, Irving confessed, was beyond him. He could only write when the mood was on him and so, utterly, "useless for regular services as an American Indian or a Don Cossack." Scott seemed to understand the case and before long, through his influential manoeuvres, the publisher Murray was found to be willing to publish Irving's work that he had earlier refused. Irving was very grateful to Scott in this preface, calling him a golden-hearted man, and Irving gives praise to Murray who became his publisher and treated him in every way in fair and "liberal spirit."

In the front of his book is a picture of the author Washington Irving in a nonchalant pose, an urbane gentleman—Charles Martin the artist, and F. Halpin the engraver. There is also a postscript at the end of this volume following the Legend of Sleepy Hollow. In this postscript we are told the story was related at a CorporateMeeting of the ancient city of Manhattoes by a shabby genteel-looking old fellow. One cautious listener declared he did not believe a word of it. And the story-teller came back with "Faith, Sir, I don't believe half of it myself."

Then, at the very end of the book is L'envoi—headed by Chaucer's poem, "Go, little book, God send thee good passage." This L'envoi closes the second volume of the London edition. The author is in an excellent frame of mind here, and tells how so many gave advice on the writing of these pages and after thinking over all the good advice he finally decided to ramble on as he had done before—and remembering that at any dinner to which guests are invited, the host serves up many different kinds of food, hoping in this way to please all. If one does not favor roast pig, then there is venison or wild-fowl, and all the fancy knick-knacks for the ladies' taste. And so the author decided to proceed with this work. He knows the many faults in it, and offering this production in a strange land is a matter to tremble for but his aim has been to please a company he has always held in awe and reverence. And so he goes ahead, "half venturing, half shrinking, surprised at his own temerity." And all found out sooner or later, that between the Preface and L'envoi there was much good material to please all kinds of people, the whole to be acclaimed a masterpiece.

L'Envoi:—

> "Go, little book, God send thee good passage—
> And speedily let this be thy prayer,
> Where thou art wrong, after their help to call,
> Thee to correct in any part or all."

> *—Chaucer—"Belle Dame Sans Merci"*

In this book the author gives an account of himself. From childhood he loved to travel about and find out things concerning people and places. He loved travel books. When grown he went about America, marvelling at its scenic beauty. And then he longed to see Europe with its treasures and romance. This country was gorgeously new looking, but Europe had all the past in its possession—even ruins held great fascination, and too, he wanted to meet the great men of the other world across the great waters. At last his wish was fulfilled and he went abroad. Every traveller then was supposed to bring back sketches in words or by pencil, views of the wonders he had met with. From his notebooks, he wonders if he wasted his time in his wanderings. He did view all the great sights, certainly. But he had heard so much about them, he took but brief notice and instead, went exploring quaint "nooks, corners, by-places."

He begins the book with the Voyage, telling what a good preparation the days at sea were. You leave your own world. Then all is quiet, nothing but sea and sky, and then, your old life is forgotten. Then you are in another world, when you land, expectant and curious about what lies around you. Then here is Rip Van Winkle, so worthily illustrated by F. O. C. Darley. Darley's bewildered Rip waking up at last to find life has passed him by.

Another essay in this book is "English Writers and American Writers," and he deplores the animosity between the two countries, going on to say that "English travelers are the best and the worst in the world." "Perhaps," he says, "the jealousies of trade, or the animosities of politics irritate." Perhaps it is our own fault, he contends, for we should have nothing to do with national prejudices. England, he reminds the reader, has ages of expression, from which we can draw golden maxims.

What an awed piece of writing Irving gives in his description of the Reading Room in the great British Library—The piece on the English Country Church has been charmingly illustrated by Darley. A Sunday in London, is another bit of vivid description—the great city hushed— the church music, like a river of joy, "elevating the great metropolis from all its sordid pollutions of the week. "And then, Sunday afternoon, with the crowds out enjoying the fresh air. His article on Westminster Abbey is interesting, built, as he tells us in 605, on the ruins of a temple to Apollo and in which St. Peter, it is claimed, appeared and consecrated it himself. Then King Edward, the Confessor, in 1045 pulled down the old church and built another. It was again modified by Henry III in 1220.

Then Irving gives us his Stratford-on-Avon and the house where Shakespeare was born and the church where he was buried. Irving concludes this survey with "Under the wizard influence of Shakespeare, I had been walking all day in a complete delusion—I had surveyed the landscape through the prism of poetry, which tinged every object with the hues of the rainbow."

In this same book, also, are the delightful tributes; "Christmas," "The Stage Coach," "Christmas Day," "The Christmas Dinner," "The Chapel of the Knights Templars," "Charter House," "Little Britain," "John Bull," Anent "John Bull," Irving says "The English excel in a certain kind of humor—which consists in caricature and giving nicknames, and they have not spared themselves." And he bids

John Bull, "Enjoy a green, an honorable, and a merry old age."

And then, back to America in this book, with "The Legend of Sleepy Hollow," its "Ichabod Crane," the long-nosed schoolmaster so well done by Darley. It was a time of tales and ghosts in particular, "The Legend of the Headless Horseman." Rebuffed by his pretty sweetheart, Ichabod on his way home on a lonely night saw a huge, misshapen creature riding along. In desperation, Ichabod lashed his stead on. Then, that dreadful Horseman tossed his head, that he had been carrying under his arm, straight at Ichabod. Crack! It struck poor Ichabod and he tumbled to the dust. His horse was found the next morning but Ichabod was never seen again in that neighborhood. An old farmer who went down to New York later heard rumors that Ichabod was still alive, that after he had left town he had prospered, studied law, and was made a Judge of the Ten Pound Court. But the old country wives say the goblins spirited him away. His rival won the pretty sweetheart and lived happily ever after. This amusing book was very popular. Its illustrations brought fame to F. O. C. Darley who was still in his twenties when he drew the pictures for it with so much care and character.

Darley's illustrations for Cooper's books were equally felicitious. As noted before, the Cooper Vignettes were Darley's pictures. These were impressed on steel by bank-note engravings, in 1862. These pictures added to the fame of Cooper's works. There was life in Darley's sketches. People were really doing things. He had caught the acting trick from his father and mother, the one-time professional actors and good ones, too. Darley could arrange groups admirably, and take care of crowds. He made a pattern for each of his pictures, and this pattern was not blatantly obvious, but pleasing. One of his special good points was the way he treated eyes, helping fix the character, speaking eyes. Looking into the pictures, the eyes there caught you, and right away you were aware of that person, and you could like or dislike what you saw reflected there. As Shakespeare says in, "Much Ado About Nothing," Let every eye negotiate for itself."

Of course, Darley, the artist, favored all the arts. He liked poetry, and his illustrations of poems were moving. His Shakespeare people were truly magnificent, tragic or humorous. In fact, all, or nearly all of Darley's pictures were poems. Two of his pictures in this present book are from his illustrations for Longfellow's, "Evangeline"—one, the dreadful expulsion:

"In silent and mournful procession
Came from the neighboring hamlets and farms the
    Arcadian women,
Driving in ponderous wains their household goods to the
    seashore—
Pausing and looking back to gaze once more on their
    dwellings,
Ere they were shut from sight by the winding road and
    the woodland.
Close at their sides their children ran, and urged on the
    oxen,
While in their little hands they clasped some fragments
    of playthings."

Darley has caught all the tragedy here in this picture he made of this sad event—the utter bewilderment and grief, the unsuspecting children, the willing oxen, and the faithful dog.

And the second picture, shows Evangeline and Basil, the blacksmith who had been with Gabriel and had sent Gabriel, his son, with hunters and trappers and Indian guides after furs. Then every day Badil and Evangeline followed on as they heard from passing Indians that Gabriel had just gone ahead.

131

"Day after day with their Indian guides,
    the maiden and Basil
Followed his (Gabriel's) flying steps, and thought each to
    o'ertake him.
Sometimes they saw, or thought they saw the smoke of his
    camp fire
Rise in the morning air from the distant plain; but at
    night,
When they had reached the place, they found only embers
    and ashes."

Darley has represented the scene so effectively. Evangeline's great disappointment, and Basil's pity as the Indian guide points to the ashes and embers. And so the quest had to continue to the heart-breaking end.

Longfellow was gracious to blacksmiths, such as Basil Lajeunnesse father of Evangeline's lover, Gabriel. Longfellow admired blacksmiths, for in this poem, "Evangeline," he tells of,

Basil, the blacksmith
Who was a mighty man in the village, and honored of
    all men;
For, since the birth of time, throughout all ages and
    nations,
Has the craft of the smith been held in repute by the
    people."

The "Village Blacksmith," pictured in this present book is probably, Longfellow's best known poem. There was the ancient Vulcan of the forge, son of Jupiter and Juno. There is the great Velasquez painting of "The Forge of Vulcan," in the museum of Madrid. And certainly Darley recognizes the worth of Longfellow. Even T. S. Eliot, in his appraisal of our earlier American literary men, admits that there was a certain dignity to Emerson and Longfellow. Darley's illustrations of Hawthorne's, "Scarlet Letter," in this distinguished work, were dedicated to Longfellow.

132

Darley could draw Indians well, too. Note the Indian guide in the "Evangeline," picture pointing to the ashes and embers. One of Darley's first triumphs was a series, "Scenes in Indian Life," done in outline, etched on stone. In "The Sketch Book," Darley has pictured King Philip, the Indian Chief. Washington Irving writing his, "Traits of Indian Character," declares the Indian was formed for the wilderness, as the Arab for the desert." Going on in this strain, Irving asserts, "There is something in the character and habits of the North American savage, taken in connection with the scenery over which he is accustomed to range, its vast lakes, boundless forests, majestic rivers, and trackless plains, that is to my mind, wonderfully striking and sublime. Dispossessed of his land, learning the vices of civilization, the red man was doubly wronged." Darley must have held the same beliefs, for he shows the Indians as superb creatures—lithe, graceful, people unlike any other nation found on this earth—their rights never respected by the white men, or rarely so.

And how magnificently Darley portrayed the glorious characters of the greatest poet of all, Shakespeare, bringing them to life with his pen and pencil, so that they acted out their parts on the pages of the book. Irving, in his article, "Westminster Abbey," dwells tenderly on the Poets Corner, illustrated in the book by Darley. Irving comments on the simplicity of the monuments, but finds that nothing unusual as the lives of poets are generally simple—"The lives of literary men afford no striking themes for the sculptor." And yet visitors seem to linger in this corner longer than in other places here given up to the great and the heroic. As Irving says, "There is "companionship between the author and the reader." In all his writings that have something to do with Shakespeare, Irving himself lingers long. Stratford-on-Avon; The Boar's Head tavern; Shakespeare's home—indeed, the whole country about here is poetic ground. "In his time, we are told, it was a popular amusement in winter evenings, to sit around the fire, and tell merry tales of errant knights, queens, lovers, lords, ladies, giants, dwarfs, thieves, cheaters, witches, fairies, goblins; and so on."

Irving has given a fine account of a Christmas Eve in England, and then came Christmas Day, and he was awakened by singing voices outside his room. As soon as he was dressed, he opened his door and found a seraph group going to each bed room, singing carols, two little girls and a boy, none over six years in age. And here Darley gives us the seraph group, suddenly abashed by being discovered so soon. Later, in a walk about the old ancestral mansion, Master Simon, some relative of the household, showed his learning in telling the newcomer from America, in the ancient and most approved treatise on hunting, one must say, "A flight of doves; or swallows; a bevy of quails; a herd of deer; a skulk of foxes; a building of rooks." An, oh, what feasting there was that day. All was merriment. Darley has drawn a group of rustic musicians serenading the Hall. And then the Christmas dinner where old English customs were kept up, even to the striking of the rolling pin by the cook on the dresser that told the servants it was time to carry in the meats and start the dinner. A long Grace, a bounteous dinner, then the cloth was removed and the wassail bowl brought in. The contents had been prepared by the Squire himself, and with apples bobbing about in the bowl. Then games and songs and jokes—such merriment. Old costumes were found, and all dressed up for a mask—a wonderful day and evening of innocent fun—old English customs still kept alive in this old mansion house.

The author makes a trip to Eastcheap to find the Boar's Head Tavern where old Jack Falstaff was wont to attend. Alas, the scene was changed from Falstaff's day. There was a picture of the Tavern in an old Church, the author was

134

told. There was a picture, not at the church, but at a tavern in the neighborhood was a box carefully kept, with a picture of the old Boar's Head Tavern on it, and two benches were produced with the names—Prince Hal and Falstaff, stamped underneath. Darley has again given this piece of writing a picture, making far-off days and people live once more in book and picture.

This Sketch Book has Chaucer's, "Go, little book," in it as noted before. Geoffrey Chaucer (1328-1400) was born in London, and died at Westminster. We are told he was the son of a vintner (according to Webster, a vintner was a wine seller, or wine merchant, especially wholesalers.) Geoffrey Chaucer served in many capacities and offices—a page—in the army—in the employ of Edward III—M.P. for Kent—, and "according to history or legend, died poor." He wrote the great, "Canterbury Tales," and, "The Legende of Goode Women," "Troylus and Criseyde," and many fine poems. He is called, "The Father of English Poetry.

Henry Wadsworth Longfellow, (1807-1882)—he was born in Portland, Maine, and attended Bowdoin College, at the same time with Nathaniel Hawthorne. He tried law, then teaching, and also literary writings, beginning to write poetry in his college days. He was a professor at Harvard. He kept up his writing until the end of his life. Who does not know his, "Psalm of Life," "The Courtship of Miles Standish," "Hiawatha," and so on. His works proved very popular. The Craigie House where he lived had at one time been the headquarters of General George Washington. Longfellow's poems were known and loved all over the world. It has been told, that when he was abroad, and was invited to visit Queen Victoria, all the kitchen maids and workers, when he appeared, crept up to take a look through peep-holes at this famous man. Queen Victoria herself was a great admirer of his. With his translations, and an imitation of old and foreign metres, he created a new influence here in his native

135

country. In 1871, he wrote, "The Divine Tragedy," a verse translation of Leiden's, "History of Christ." "Evangeline," written in 1849, is in dactylic hexameters. This is an unrhymed poem, every line with five dactyls, (one long and two short syllables) and one trochaic (a long and a short syllable). Here is such a line below:

> "This is the forest primeval. The murmuring pines and the hemlocks."

Brander Matthews, in his, "Study of Versification," page 187, believes this is the perfect meter for "Evangeline," and Matthews here quotes from Oliver Wendell Holmes, "The poet knows better than his critics the length of step which best befits his muse." James Brander Matthews, (1852-1929), was born in New Orleans. He graduated from Columbia in 1872, and became professor there of literature in 1892. In 1922-24, he was chancellor of the American Academy of Arts and Letters. He also served as president of the National Institute of Arts and Letters, (1913-14).

Oliver Wendell Holmes, (1809-94), was born at Cambridge, Massachusetts, and graduated from Harvard in 1829. He studied medicine at the Harvard Medical School. He was, "The Autocrat at the Breakfast Table," in the Atlantic Monthly, 1857. He published novels and essays, and many poems, among these, "Old Ironsides"; "The One Hoss Shay"; etc.; etc.

Brander Matthews, in his "A Study of Versification," tells that Longfellow tried another meter for "Evangeline," rimed pentameters, five feet of one short and one long syllable each, with the matter practically the same. But the whole effect was ruined, and he went back to his original dactylic hexameter. Page 136 of Brander Matthews' "A Study of Versification," records that Oliver Wendell Holmes, in his paper, "Physiology of Versification," worked out that as the average man breathes twenty times a minute and the tetrameter goes at the same rate, we are told here that, the average man in a minute will read aloud about twenty lines of Hiawatha, which is in the four-measure meter. The tetrameter thus—"But the farther Hiawatha," but this makes for sing-song with its "fatal facility," Dr. Holmes said that iambic pentameter line will be read at the rate of fourteen lines a minute. Emerson quotes Shakespeare's view, "The thought constructs the tune." And reading to get the sense of the line will bring out the rhythm. Dr. Holmes said he did not believe any other measure but the hexameter could have told the lovely story of Evangeline, as well. This was the English hexameter with strict rules. We must remember that "Evangeline," came out in 1847, and when Darley made the illustrations for it, was still new and very popular.

CHAPTER X

For Good and All

PHILADELPHIA, where Darley was born, had the first magazine in this country, (1741), and the first daily newspaper here, (1784). When William Penn founded this place, he declared he wanted it to be a, "green country town." Penn made friends with the Indians. Small wonder that Darley had kind feelings toward the Indians, and drew them so worthily. As mentioned earlier, Thomas Sully, (1783-1872), the portrait painter, born in England, but came to America and proved very successful in Philadelphia, was connected with the Darley family. This Thomas Sully was greatly influenced by Sir Thomas Lawrence, (1769-1830), the renowned English portrait painter. He succeeded Sir Joshua Reynolds as the painter to the King in 1792, and was knighted, 1815, a fashionable painter, and his studies of children were the vogue. He did, "Pinkie," now in the Huntington Gallery. Among Lawrence's pictures of grown people was his famous painting of Mrs. Siddons (in the National Gallery, London). Sarah Kemble Siddons, (1755-1831), was the English actress belonging to the well-known stage family. Mrs. Siddons played many of Shakespeare's great roles,— Desdemona, Ophelia, Lady Macbeth. Among the many portraits done of her, was Sir Joshua Reynolds' famous portrait as, "The Tragic Muse." George III was ruling then in Great Britain.

We can see that Darley had as background, people who were talented and worthily ambitious. Philadelphia was a good starting point, as it was always known as a culture center. And 1822 was an excellent time to come into this exciting world here in the U.S.A. with James Monroe, President, in the "Era of Good Feeling." This bright youngest child of the Darley family had some good fairies as godparents, giving him as birthday presents, a keen eye, a kindly heart, a self-reliant but modest spirit, all to prove of great value to the new little boy in the Darley family.

It seems strange that the Darleys located in Philadelphia, for that town had formerly been harshly against the members of the acting profession. But, of course, by the time Felix Darley was born, both mother and father had given up acting, and then, too, the English soldiers stationed in Philadelphia during the Revolution had done much to break down such prejudice, constantly putting on and acting in shows of their own, to lighten the dreary winter months of enforced idleness. Agnes Repplier, the essayist, tells of these entertainments in her book, "Philadelphia, the Place and the People." One of her pieces of information here, is that Major Andre had created such a beautifully painted drop curtain for the improvised stage. He must have been something of an artist, too. And, then, the Darleys might have had relatives in Philadelphia, and so directed them there when new-comers in this country. The artist, John Sully, who lived there was some connection of theirs.

What a strange assortment of different kinds of people a city can hold. Philadelphia had Benjamin Franklin, Benedict Arnold, who brought his bride to live there, and Evangeline Bellefontaine and Gabriel Lajeunesse meeting in the last dim days again in the old Alms House,—Betsy Ross, Washington, the President, and so on. Sully came to this country when he was nine years old, and spent most of his days there. Philadelphia had always been opposed to slavery, and it is said, that the reason the Government was moved to Washington was because there was so much opposition to the

Philadelphia Quaker Abolitionists. Philadelphia was General McClellan's birthplace. President Lincoln's body was brought to Philadelphia and rested in state for two days in Independence Hall. The Centennial in Philadelphia, in 1876, was the first World's Fair in this country. There had never been such heat as experienced during the time of the Centennial Exposition, from May to November, with the thermometer registering each day from ninety degrees to one hundred and two.

At the time of the Centennial there were thirty-six States in the Union. Mrs. Gillespie, in her book, "A Book of Remembrance," Chapters XVIII, XIX, tells of the great work done by the women of Philadelphia in organizing the Centennial Exposition. All the women throughout the United States joined in helping Philadelphia with this mighty event, even to erecting a splendid building to show the women's exhibits. Darley had a painting in this great Fair, "A Street Scene in Rome." This picture was enthusiastically received, and later purchased. The general concensus was that this Centennial Exposition not only proved what the nation had accomplished in one hundred years, but also what it should strive for in the future, "to grow up and learn a lesson from the old world, in all the arts and sciences."

Certainly the observant and open-minded Darley must have been taught much as he went through the buildings there, especially the Art Exhibit. He never stopped learning. But he had faith in this Country, a true American, not too proud for everyday work, but eager to reach the top, never ceasing in his efforts toward perfection. At fourteen, precocious and mature, Darley went to work—not much money at home, evidently. Did he find work as an office boy or an errand runner dreary? He knew how to lighten dull days. Maybe not during office hours, as he must have been kept busy, but in the long evenings, with no extra spending money for outside entertainment, he started drawing things to please himself. He did not waste his talent. His family and friends liked what he drew. So these sketches found a way into the magazines—the Godey Book and similar, always ready for an opportunity to do something worthwhile.

An order came in for a series of Scenes of Indian Life. He was born a hundred and fifty years ago, or thereabouts, and as a boy, Philadelphia could not have been too cityfied as yet, and there must have still been Indians living on the outskirts, and coming into town at times. Penn, the founder, had always treated the Indians so well, there never had been any trouble. The Indians were free to come and go unmolested. Darley must have been friendly with them, and he pictured them as handsome creatures, active, graceful, devoted when sure of sincerity. He represented them more creditably than he did the rude, rough Yankee sharpers he was called on to portray, in American fiction.

Sylvester Judd's story, "Margaret," had much idealism to it, and it appealed so to Darley, that quietly by himself, he took to setting down portions of this tale, in drawings. When these sketches finally came to public notice, and were acclaimed, then Darley moved on to New York, to enter upon his great period as an illustrator par excellence.

Wanted by the best publishers and authors, both here and abroad, he was a professional and was elected to the National Academy of Design, where he regularly exhibited. Another kind of drawing that he must have liked for the vignettes for bank notes of Japan (Nippon). This Nippon was founded, according to tradition, in 660 B.C. by the Emperor Jimmu, a descendant of the Sun goddess. The Portuguese were the first Europeans to visit Japan in 1542. Then St. Francis Xavier, the Jesuit missionary, introduced Christianity in 1549. Then in 1854, in President's Pierce's term of office, Commodore Perry opened up Japan to western connections. This Commodore Matthew Calbraith Perry, (1794-1858), in 1853-54, went with a fleet to Japan, and

141

managed to secure a treaty from the Japanese Government, opening up Japanese ports to the U.S. trade. His brother was the famous naval officer, Oliver Hazard Perry, (1785-1819). The British at Lake Erie surrendered to him, September 10, 1813, and then he sent in his well-known report, "We have met the enemy, and they are ours."

Doing banknote vignettes for the Japanese Government must have been interesting to Darley who could appreciate the refinement of Japanese Art. And the Japanese, in turn, prized his fine line drawings. Like the Japanese, Darley took delight in the dramatic and picturesque aspects of art.

As the various new books came out, or old favorites reissued at popular demand, Darley was commissioned to illustrate these volumes, and he did the work so well, they have remained timeless. Look at other and later illustrations, such as those of Charles Dana Gibson, or almost any one of the once popular artists, and we smile at them for their dated appearance. Real people are not in such pictures at all, but simply models dressed in outmoded styles that could never have been lovely. But with Darley, there is a difference, an originality that interests us immediately, much as in Hogarth's or Cruikshank's, and yet so utterly unlike these pictures. These are not simply illustrations, these are interpretation of character. George Cruickshank, (1792-1878), was the English illustrator. He did, "Grimms' Fairy Tales," and, "The Life of John Falstaff," and Dickens' "Oliver Twist." Darley did not use as much caricature, although he could do it if he wanted to, and extremely well. But all his drawings were nothing out of the ordinary. Simple and quaint as they are, they prove as enjoyable today as when they first were made.

There is even something of Blake in Darley's pictures— a certain innocence and freshness, as if the people and scenes he showed had been allowed to return to some Garden of Eden for the time being. And yet they are so real, people in exceptional moments perhaps, not fully realizing these moments are exceptional. William Blake (1767-1827), the English poet, painter and engraver, and a visionary. Swinburne wrote his Life, Blake illustrated, "The Book of Job." His best known short poem is, perhaps, "Tiger, Tiger." Algernon Charles Swinburne, (1837-1909), an English critic as well as a poet, but some of his poems are too mechanical and too ornate. Darley evolved in his work and life, going step by step into new worlds of discovery and adventure. Surely he must have found much difference between "The Village Blacksmith," and "Tristram Shandy," to say nothing of Shakespeare.

Today with so few horses in use, except for sport or pleasure, the blacksmith has become almost a joke, a thing of the past, and yet, in his day he was a man of importance, and a very necessary person. Darley has represented him at his best, a craftsman of high order, and, Darley doing this has opened our eyes, taught us something. The forge with its fiery background has awe and mystery about it. We spoke before of Vulcan's Forge of old mythology. In Velasquez's picture in the Museum of Madrid, Spain, "The Forge of Vulcan," we see this god at work. Vulcan fashioned golden palaces for all the gods on Mount Olympus. He is the patron of blacksmiths and artists.

> "Those who labor
> The sweaty forge, who edge the crooked scythe,
> Bend stubborn steel, and harden gleaming armor,
> Acknowledge Vulcan's aid."
>
> *Pryor*

Matthew Pryor, (1664-1721) was the English poet and wit. He wrote, "The City Mouse," and, "The Country Mouse," and also light verse. He was a diplomat, and helped arrange the Peace of Utrecht ending the War of the Spanish Succession, (1713).

After Darley became recognized for his work, he was kept busy by Harper's, Appleton's, and all the important publishing houses that used illustrations in their books. An Anthology, that Appleton's brought out in 1950, to celebrate the One Hundred and Twenty-fith Anniversary of the foundation of D. Appleton & Company, has an interesting title, "Fruit Among the Leaves," and is a play on the name, "Appleton." "Inter Folia Fructus," (Fruit Among the Leaves), was the motto that went with the picture of an apple tree, becoming the mark of the publishing house. Samuel Chew tells in the history of the publishing house of one of these books, named," The Hive of the Bee-Hunter," A Repository of Sketches including, Peculiar American Scenery and Rural Sports," 1854, by Thomas Bangs Thorpe of Louisiana. There is humor here as well as imagination, and it is illustrated by Darley, having in it nine Sporting Prints.

James Fenimore Cooper was still very popular, although dead twenty years, and the Appletons brought out in 1872 a complete edition, with illustrations by F. O. C. Darley. Another Appleton book was, "Picturesque America, the Land We Live In," 1872, and Darley's, "Buffalo Hunt," is an illustration in this series, and so vividly pictured in an idealized, unromantic way.

In the front of the book, "Fruit Among the Leaves," is a resume of the book company through one hundred and twenty-five years, and this is the way it reads—D. Appleton and Company, 1825-1933; The Century Company, 1870 to 1933; F. S. Crofts, Inc. 1924-1947; D. Appleton, Century-Crofts, Inc. 1933-1948. The Appletons also did, "Alice in Wonderland," with illustrations by Tenniel. John Tenniel, (1820-1904). (Sir John Tenniel) was the English artist and caricaturist, best known for his pictures in, "Alice in Wonderland," and "Alice Through the Looking-Glass," and Thomas Moore's, "Lalla Rookh."

Thomas Moore (1779-1852), was the Irish English poet.

144

His Irish melodies are well-known—"Believe Me if All Those Endearing Young Charms," "Oft in a Stilly Night," and many others. He wrote the poetic romance, Lalla Rookh," 1817. This was an Oriental romance. He traveled in the United States in 1814. Lalla Rookh was his most successful work.

In connection with that Sporting Series, we do not believe that Darley's gentle spirit was in it. Hunting may be all right when necessary, but when it become simply sport, surely it is as cruel as bull-fighting that civilized people deplore. Of course there are no buffalos left to hunt now. And what sport was there in fishing with a bow and arrow? It would seem that Darley tried to soften the horror of buffalo hunting in the picture that he drew for this series. He always did eyes so well, and this time he puts in the upturned look of the falling buffalo an almost human appeal for pity. Darley did noble work with his drawings of Washington, and of Nathan Hale, noble subjects.

The English, too, had their hero, Major Andre. Through the treachery of Benedict Arnold, West Point, that most strategic point, was to fall into the hands of the enemy. After Andre's capture, we read in Weir Mitchell's book, "Hugh Wynne, Quaker," how this Quaker tried to get Andre's death sentence lightened, to a less severe punishment. A friend of Washington, Hugh Wynne brought letters of appeal to Washington. The great man, though over-burdened with work, received Wynne, and read the letters. When he looked up at last, the book tells us, "The General's eyes overflowed." But there was nothing he could do. And we learn when Andre was led to the gallows, "he looked very white in his red coat." But he thanked Wynne and all those on hand for what they tried to do, and went forward steadfastly to his doom.

In the Anniversary Anthology of the Appletons, for which Darley did such good work, there appears on page

145

157, of this Anthology, five colophons representing the five stages of this publishing house. A colophon, according to Webster's Dictionary, is a Latin word taken from the Greek, and it means an emblem, usually a device assumed by the publishing house, placed on the title page or at the end of a book. The Appleton Publishing House used an apple tree as a play on the name of the firm. The colophons represented the changes in the firm.

In his early days in the 1800's, Washington Irving, weary of the pompous style of writing then in vogue, decided to parody this style in, "A History of New York." At first he intended a complete history, then finding that too much, decided to write only about New York, or New Amsterdam, to give it its name under the Dutch Rule. He had found out that the people of his day knew little or nothing about the charming and poetical period of Dutch occupation with its jollifications, customs, and oddities. So he wrote the comic history. It is supposed to have been written by a M. Deidrich Knickerbocker, and published by the unpaid landlord of the hotel where Knickerbocker had stayed and who had found the manuscript after the old fellow had disappeared. The landlord had advertised, asking news of said Knickerbocker, but had no word of him. However the History found so much favor with the descendants of the Dutch, that the old fellow was discovered at last in a country retreat, and, as the author, was given many a rousing cheer. There was even bestowed on him a little house in a rural district, this house given by an admirer of his writings and who was a descendant of the Dutch settlers. But Knickerbocker did not live long to enjoy his success. And so he died soon.

Irving starts Book I with the history of New Amsterdam all mixed up with the creation of the world. This was all written in 1809, when Irving was about twenty-six years old. It had been favorably received but, of course, not widely known. So, in 1848, he re-wrote it all, adding to some parts,

146

and abstracting from others. And in 1849-50, it was Darley who designed the pictures for it, the sketches that pleased Irving so much, saying to his nephew, Pierre Irving, "Darley hit it in the illustrated History of New York. Jarvis tried, but failed to embody my conception of Diedrich Knicker-bocker, and Leslie also."

Jarvis and Leslie were the two well-known artists whose services were then very much in demand. Needless to say, as everyone knows, this book has been widely acclaimed and is still a required piece of writing. Irving's, "History of New York," has been issued many times. In 1886, the Grolier Club brought out an edition of one hundred and seventy-five copies in two volumes, with illustrations by George H. Boughton, Will H. Drake, and Howard Pyle, and etchings by Henry C. Eno and F. Raubicheck.

The Grolier Club, an association of lovers of fine books, in New York City, has itself issued books on typography, book-binding, and other like matters. This Club was named for Jean Grolier de Servieres, vicomte d'Aguisy, (1479-1565) who was born at Lyons, and became a famous book collector. He started his collection in Italy. His library was estimated to contain over three thousand choice volumes, a great library for those days.

As told before, Darley later did numerous illustrations for James Fenimore Cooper's famous works. Darley headed the list of illustrators in those days. With so much to do, one wonders how he acomplished so much and so well. He must have been a tremendous worker, early and late. And yet he seemed to thrive on this industry, never satisfied with anything less than perfection, or as near to his idea as he could make it.

Many would marvel if they heard that Noah had any-thing to do with America. But Diedrich Knickerbocker goes on to explain, that after the flood, Noah, sole proprietor of the earth, gave Asia to his son, Shem; and to his son, Ham,

147

Africa, and to his son, Japhet, Europe. And old Knicker-bocker bewails the fact that Noah had but three sons. If there had been a fourth son, of course, this one would have been awarded, yes, America. So that was why America was so long being discovered. And yet, there are those who do believe that Noah himself discovered this country and the Ark landed here.

However, Knickerbocker declares he will accept the vulgar opinion that Christopher Colon, or Columbus, dis-covered this wonderful land, on October 12, 1492. And then, later, the Dutch were here, and dedicated Manhattoes to good St. Nicholas. And in this vein, Knickerbocker rambles on, philosophizing and prattling on all matters. For instance, he attempts to prove, as if it were necessary, that all creatures have their uses. For example flies, that are abhorred, are food for spiders, thus doing away with them. And spiders, in turn, are done away with by a higher species of insect. And so it goes. Knickerbocker tells of the little group of Dutchmen starting out from Pavonia, and going up the East River, until getting into the turmoil of Hell Gate, were all but lost, but saved just in time by some sage Dutch advice. And then, as to the etymology of the name, "Manhattoes." Some believe the name originated in the custom of the squaws in wearing men's hats, hence, Man-hat-on. Another version was, and a good one, that the Indians called the place, "Mannahata," meaning "The Island of Manna, a land flowing with milk and honey." We learn from the worthy Knickerbocker that the Dutchmen pondered just what name to give this fine Island of Manhattoes, for Manhattoes was simply heathenish rubbish. And at length, a very bright one startled them all by declaring the new name would be nothing less than New Amsterdam. What a wonderful idea! And such was the name until the English came to travel and see the world. They brought with them ideas of refinement and culture.

148

In time, there were the big days of expansion—The Crystal Palace in London; the Paris Exposition; and The Centennial Exposition in Philadelphia. Libraries sprang up; art museums and academies started; population was spreading far and wide; cities grew amazingly; parks were opened; times were flourishing here generally; the nation was destined for greatness. Yes, that is America's destiny. It will not last forever. Every nation has its Golden Age, and then begins, slowly or quickly, to deteriorate. In Darley's time, the United States was coming forward, fast and faster, but always with the awful blot of slavery, like a dark shadow over the land. Then, finally the cruel Civil War, with its needless waste of lives. And after that, poverty for the South, and prosperity for the North. Great events kept happening, like Perry's opening of Japan and we became aware of art. The Metropolitan Museum opened in 1870, with Egyptian mummies and lore that visitors looked on with awe. Important visitors came this way, and lectured and read and sang and acted for us.

Yes, those last twenty to twenty-five years of his life, must have been very happy ones for F. O. C. Darley, and he went on living, quietly, gently out in his pleasant country home in Delaware. And, then, without any warning, the newspapers of March 28, 1888, on the front pages carried, the news that Artist Darley was dead. Sad news for a Wednesday, the day the Sun was made. Death came on him unexpectedly, the day before, March 27th, at his home. A heart attack was the physician's verdict, an easy and quick way to go. He was sixty-six years old according to the calendar, but he had really lived several life-times with his extraordinary development, working from comics straight on to Shakespeare. The New York Times called him, "the celebrated designer and illustrator," and went on to tell of his great pictures for Washington Irving's and Fenimore Cooper's works, and Shakespeare's. The obituary of Felix Octavius Carr Darley

149

in the Philadelphia Telegraph was reprinted in "American Architects and Building News," April 14, 1888. Besides The New York Times, the New York Tribune, and the New York Post printed eulogistic obituaries for Darley on March 28, 1888.

No one, since then, has come forward to pull down his fame in any degree. He still remains the foremost illustrator of his time, and his pictures are still a delight today. Was he satisfied with what he had accomplished? Probably he was not. Chaucer says, "The life so short the craft so long to learn."

BOOKS READ

James Fenimore Cooper, by James Grossman (The American Men of Letters Series), William Sloane Associates, 1949.

Mark Twain's, *Literary Offenses of Fenimore Cooper,"* 1895, North American Review, July. Also in Edmund Wilson's, *The Shock of Recognition,* 1943. Doubleday, Doran & Co. Garden City, N. Y.

Art in America, by Suzanne LaFolette, Harper & Brothers, New York and London, 1929 (MCMXXIX).

Fenimore Cooper, Critic of His Times, by Robert Edward Spiller, N.Y., 1931, N. Y. Minton, Balch & Company.

The Sea Lions or the Lost Sealers; by J. Fenimore Cooper, illustrated by Darley, Townsend & Co., New York, 1860.

The Chain Bearer, or the Little Page Manuscripts, by J. Fenimore Cooper, Illustrated by Darley. New York, Townsend, 1860.

Afloat and Ashore, A Sea Tale, by J. Fenimore Cooper, illustrated by Darley, New York, Townsend, 1861.

American Artists, Royal Cortissoz, 1923.

Art in America, by S. G. W. Benjamin, New York, Harper Brothers, Publishers, 1880.

Tristram Shandy, by Laurence Sterne.

Pictorial History of the Civil War in the United States, by Benson John Lossing. 1868.

Life & Letters of Washington Irving, by his nephew, Pierre M. Irving, 1862, G. P. Putnam.

Samuel F. B. Morse, Letters and Journals by Edward Lind Morse (son), Houghton Mifflin Company, Boston and New York, 1914.

Oliver W. Larkin, *Samuel F. B. Morse and American Democratic Art,* edited by Oscar Handlin, Little Brown and Company, Boston, Toronto, 1954.

The Life of S. T. Coleridge, by Lawrence Handon, New York, Oxford University Press, 1939.

The Lady of Godey's—Sarah Josepha Hale, By Ruth E. Finley, Philadelphia and London, J. B. Lippincott Company, 1931.

American Graphic Art, by F. Weitenkampf, New York, 1912, Henry Holt & Co.

Christmas Stories, by Edward Everett Hale, Boston, Little, Brown & Company, 1909.

Advertising Directory," New York As It Is," 1833, Edited by Edwin William published by J. Desturnell, 155 Broadway, New York City.

Wilson's Business Directory—1872-73, The Trow City Directory Company, 52 Greene Street, New York City.

Doggett's New York City Directory, 1849-1850. Jogn Doggett, Jr., & Co., 64 Liberty Street, Sandstone Buildings.

I Remember, by J. Henry Harper, Harper Harper & Brothers, New York, 1934.

Raymond of the Times, by Francis Browne.

The Shock of Recognition, by Edmond Wilson, 1943.

Philadelphia, the Place and the People, by Agnes Repplier, 1898. Macmillan Co.

Fruit Among the Leaves, An Anthology, 1950, New York, One hundred and twenty-fifth anniversary of D. Appleton & Company.

A Book of Remembrance, by Mrs. E. D. Gillespie, Philadelphia & London, J. R. Lippincott Company, 1901.

The History of the Ideals of American Art, by Eugene Neuhaus.

The Pocket History of American Painting, by James Thomas Flexner.

Guerber's Myths of Greece and Rome, American Book Company, New York, Cincinnati, Chicago, 1893.

Hartman, *A History of American Art,* Little, Page & Co., Boston, 1911.

Book of the Arts, by Henry T. Tuckerman, New York, G. P. Putnam, & Son, 1867.

Occasional Dottings by the Wayside, by T. S. Cummings, New York, 1826-1885.

Book of the Artists. American Artist Life, by Henry Tuckerman, G. P. Putnam & Co.

152

INDEX

INDEX—*Continued*